AN AMATEUR'S GUIDE TO THE PURSUIT OF HAPPINESS

Britt Reints

Printed in the United States

First printing, 2013

ISBN 978-0-9896738-0-8
Library of Congress Control Number: 2013945251

Credits:
Cover Design: Greta Polo - design.gretapolo.net
Cover image: © Tryfonov - Fotolia.com

"Refreshing, practical, honest. These words are for Britt as an author and for this book, which is a powerful nudge and great resource for anyone who wants to be happier."

--Nataly Kogan, Co-founder & Chief Happiness Officer at Happier, Inc.

"A surprisingly blunt look at the reality we are all living. We all crave to be happier, but few books lay out the hardships, sacrifices and self determination it takes to actually achieve it. A simple step-by-step guide this book isn't, but an honest guide to getting started with a happier life it is!"

--C.C. Chapman, Author of
Amazing Things Will Happen

"Britt is a wealth of knowledge in this new book on one of my favorite topics — happiness! In this book, you'll find inspiration empowerment, actionable tips and strategies, everything you need to know to start your happiness journey. Congrats on a relatable, candid and great read."

--Erica Diamond, Founder and Editor-In-Chief
WomenOnTheFence.com®

For Jared, Devin, and Emma.
Thank you for being the North Star, full moon,
and rising sun along my journey.

Contents

"I suggest that the only books that influence us are those for which we are ready, and which have gone a little further down our particular path than we have yet gone ourselves."

-E.M. Forster

Introduction

There are a lot of ideas out there about what will make you happy. You can buy books that will tell you exactly what you should do from the moment you get up in the morning until you close your eyes at night, books written by well-meaning, self-aware people. You can also watch documentaries, read magazine articles, and study the results of scientific research. There's just one problem: none of those authors, gurus, or scientists have met you.

I probably haven't met you either. Even if we had met, I lack the ability to crawl inside your head and dig into your heart, which is ultimately what's required to "find happiness." So, I am not going to tell you what, exactly, will make you happy. The cold, hard truth is that you have to figure that out for yourself.

But that doesn't mean you're in this alone.

I can't tell you exactly what to do, but I can give you some guidance so that you can find your own path to happiness. In fact, I'll offer you five different maps that you can use to pursue your version of happiness.

What Is Happiness?

The words happy and happiness can be used to describe so many things, and if we aren't clear about what we mean, it's easy to dismiss its importance or dodge the work required to experience it. "No one is happy all the time," you might say when you find yourself bumping up against an uncomfortable question. And no, no one is smiling, or laughing, or feeling jovial all the time. (Actually, allowing yourself to feel unhappy is an essential step towards finding happiness.) But still, we seem to know instinctively that happiness – whatever it is – is something worth pursuing.

In *The Happiness Myth*, author Jennifer Michael Hecht defines three types of happiness: a moment of happiness, a good day, and a happy life. Hecht suggests that no further definition is needed because the difference between the three is obvious when we use or hear the word happiness in context. However, she points out that these three types of happiness are rarely in harmony with each other, which can make achieving happiness more difficult than defining it. "Anything we do," Hecht writes, "may facilitate one kind of happiness and inhibit another." In other words, skipping work to see a movie may help you have a good day but interfere with your ability to have a happy life. This conflict can complicate things when you're trying to define happiness for yourself.

Nataly Kogan, CEO of a company called Happier that created a mobile app to help people track their happiness moments, prefers the term "happier" to "happy" or "happiness". "Happy insinuates a nirvana state that you arrive at," Nataly says, "and that doesn't exist." I tend to agree with this philosophy; happiness is not a destination, but rather a direction in which you head or a manner in which you travel. What most of us are seeking is not to capture happiness, but to experience being happier. Being happier, then, is an effort to move forward, to be a little farther down the path than you were yesterday.

But there's more. As much as being happier is about going somewhere, journeying forward, we also want to feel like we're already in the right place. Surely that sense of contentment is also a part of happiness.

My personal definition of happiness includes a description from Christian scripture. Happiness is a calm deep in my soul, a "peace that passes all understanding." The goal of this book is to help you find that peace, along with a sense of progress and moments of joy on the journey.

Should We Pursue Happiness?

For many of us, the pursuit of happiness is complicated by our fear that wanting to be happy makes us selfish jerks. We worry that our wants and needs are too small or too big or too frivolous or too... something that would make us not OK.

It is more than OK to pursue your own happiness.

In her 2011 commencement speech at UC Berkley, sociologist Christine Carter told graduates that their responsibility now was to, "go out into the world and create a life in which you are happy." She then explains, "I am not telling you to go out and be selfish. Don't make the mistake that many people do, and confuse gratification or worldly pleasures with the stuff that truly makes up a meaningful, happy life. I am telling you to go out and create a happy life because I believe that this is the first and the best way to make the world a better place."

I wholeheartedly agree with Dr. Carter. Our individual happiness makes the world better in numerous ways. People who are happy are more likely to be successful, to give to charity, and to serve their communities. Relationship experts tell us that taking responsibility for our own happiness improves our interactions with other people. Also, our happiness creates a ripple effect among the people we know. Studies have shown that one person's happiness spreads not only to their friends, but their friends' friends, and their friends' friends' friends. That's three degrees of happiness that can be tangibly traced.

Your happiness matters, in other words. It matters in your own life and it matters in the lives of the people with whom you interact. And it is most certainly worth pursuing. When you hear the call to happiness, it is your responsibility to answer it.

Besides, what's the alternative? Are you supposed to pretend not to be looking for happiness while secretly hoping it will find you? That sort of insincere self deception can't possibly be good for you. Forget about science or logic; your gut tells you that you were made for more than that.

The Five Maps Of Happiness

If happiness is a journey, it makes sense to have a map. You may even need more than one. But, remember what a map can – and cannot – do for you.

Although we use maps to guide us on our journeys, a map itself prescribes no route. It is merely a representation of the landscape, a way of looking at what's ahead so that you might decide for yourself where you're going and how to get there. Open a map of the United States and you will see state lines and road markings, but there is no itinerary without your input. You'll find a globe, a city map, or even the amusement park map you get at the turnstile to be just as impartial. Instead of instructions, what these different maps offer are new suggestions about how to look at the world around you. These varying perspectives do not change the landscape itself, but they hint at new ways you might choose to navigate it.

In this book, I've outlined five different maps of happiness. They are meant to help you look at the world around you a little differently. Approaching your own life through the filter of any of these maps will help you discern what happiness means to you and let you enjoy being happier.

The five maps in this book are:

- **Personal Responsibility** – find the line between what you can control and what you can't.

- **Growth** – learn to create sustainable newness, which is proven to be a happiness booster.

- **Gratitude** – learn to recognize and appreciate all that you already have.

- **Self Discovery** – better understand who you are so that you can figure out what you need to be happy.

- **Acceptance** - embrace what is without judgment to experience peace and happiness.

These maps were forged from my own life lessons and from the sweat, tears, and courage of dozens of other people who have fallen and gotten back up and been generous with their stories and lessons. The maps are the culmination of navel gazing, girl talk, and lots of billable hours. You will read a few words from experts, but mostly - as with any map - the lines are drawn from human experience in a humble attempt to make clearer the way for anyone who might come later.

None of these maps provides a singular route to happiness, because there is no such thing. There are different approaches you can take and multiple paths that can lead you to being happier tomorrow than you are today. The happiness maps offered here will not determine your journey or your specific destination, but they can light your way. Each will offer a new representation of the landscape, a way of looking at what's behind, around, and ahead of you so that you might recognize the next best step to take.

This book doesn't contain an exhaustive list of the various routes to happiness; there is no exhaustive list of ways to look at, think about, approach, or achieve happiness. The possibilities are endless. No one should ever hope to find all the answers in one book any more than one person should aspire to learn all of the lessons in one life. It is a place to start. A nudge. An attempt to shine enough light on the path so that you might have the courage to take your next step. It is, I hope, a beginning.

You can read this book from beginning to end in sequential order, or start with the map that sounds most interesting to you. Think of this as a choose-your-own-adventure book about happiness.

As you read through each section, you may find that some of the ideas feel like common sense and others make you supremely uncomfortable. The ones you hate may well be the ones that would make the biggest difference if applied to your life; our brains have a strange habit of hating the things we need most (like Brussels sprouts, flossing, and confrontation). My greatest hope is that you'll discover something here that excites you, makes you believe you can be happy, and helps you take a step forward.

In the end, you may find you need to create your own map. I believe this book will help you do that, too.

Who The Heck Am I?

I'm a woman who has fallen on her face a lot. In the process of picking myself up, I've developed an obsession with happiness and the courage it takes to pursue it. I've learned a lot, and I want to share some of that with you.

There was a time when I had everything a woman my age could want. I owned two homes, drove a new vehicle, had a decent-paying job, and my family - one husband, two kids, one cat - could have starred in a Kleenex commercial. I taught religious education and organized the annual Fall Festival at our church. I volunteered as a drill team coach at the local high school. My entire extended family lived within a two-hour radius, and my best friend from high school lived one block away. I had everything the studies said should make me happy, and I was miserable. I wondered what was wrong with me.

How could my seemingly perfect life be so unfulfilling? I loved my husband, adored my kids and enjoyed my home, but I was walking around with a giant hole in me all the time. I went to church and volunteered in my community, but that just made me feel like a fraud and even more guilty about not being happy. I changed jobs. I made new friends. I sought new hobbies and lost 30 pounds. I even tried moving to a sunnier state, but I was still incomplete.

Then, in what can only be described as a fit of desperation, I blew up my life.

I turned my back on what my church, my parents and my friends had said was right and instead embraced a second adolescence. I went out to bars on weeknights while my husband stayed home with the kids. I threw myself into becoming an Internet pseudo-celebrity. I broke promises, shattered vows, and flirted with the idea of packing up and leaving my family behind. Instead, I asked my husband, Jared, to move out and told him I wanted a divorce.

I knocked down every moral pillar I'd ever erected and found myself standing in a smoldering pile of rubble. And, for the first time in my life, I finally felt free. I could, at last, hear my own voice loud and clear.

I had always been good at clearing the slate. I suspect I was an arsonist in a past life and that I'd carried those smash and burn tendencies with me into this one. When life wasn't going the way I wanted it to, or it was and I was still inexplicably unhappy, my instinct was to set a match to the familiar and do my best to burn the whole damn thing down. I had quit jobs without having backup plans. I'd moved to new houses or new states. I had walked away from hard relationships and attempted to replace them with brand new ones. I'd tried to start my life over in a dozen ways before, but this time was different.

By the time I kicked my husband out of the house, I had done such a thorough job of destroying not just the external trappings of my life, but the inner fiber of who I thought I was, that I didn't have the first clue how to go about rebuilding myself from scratch.

That's when my happiness journey started.

My first step was self-destruction. My next was to hire a therapist to help me decide if I did, in fact, want to get a divorce. She taught me how to appreciate and prioritize my own happiness, reassess my values, and recognize the difference between what I believe and what I'd been taught to believe. I found the courage to say I could be happy getting divorced, and then the strength to ask my husband for forgiveness when I realized that I didn't really want one.

Because I am the luckiest woman in the world, Jared agreed to move back home and go to marriage counseling, an idea we'd kicked around hypothetically for years but had always put off because it seemed like a frivolous expense. (Incidentally, I got pregnant the first time because I thought birth control was too expensive. I am clearly not a good judge of what constitutes a frivolous expense.) We worked with an incredibly gifted counselor who taught us how to take responsibility for ourselves instead of each other and how to listen. Our relationship was so drastically transformed through counseling that we begged our therapist to let us continue long after she tried to kick us out. We agreed to less frequent sessions, but only gave up marriage counseling completely when the next step on our happiness journey made office visits impossible.

In 2011, Jared and I made the completely insane decision to move into an RV with our two kids. We sold our home in Florida, gave away my car, held garage sales to get rid of everything else, and then spent 10 months driving around the United States. The adventure taught us the power of change, courage, and doing the things everyone says are crazy.

In the summer of 2012, we moved to Pittsburgh. We'd fallen in love with the city when we'd visited it as part of our great American road trip, and we wanted to live in a place that we loved (and could afford). Today, we're still pursuing happiness with gusto, but our lives look nothing like a commercial. We live in a three-bedroom duplex, where I work as a freelance writer. We own one 10-year-old vehicle (the same one we took around the country), and we do most of our shopping at the local thrift stores. We keep in touch with our family via Skype and are trying to make new friends while volunteering at the kids' school. Our life isn't perfect, but it fits. And I am, without a doubt, more happy than not.

I recommend you avoid following in my footsteps as much as possible.

You do not need to decimate your existing life in order to have a happier one. Of course, sometimes life gets rebooted for us. Sometimes rock bottom comes not because we are reincarnated arsonists, but because life has a funny way of sending us back to start when we need it, whether we want it or not.

And sometimes we just decide it's time to make a change.

Whether your journey to happiness is prompted by self-sabotage, unforeseen tragedy, or a quiet yearning for more, what matters is that you face the path in front of you as navigator. Regardless of how you got to this place of new beginnings, it's up to you to decide where to go from here.

But how? When everything we've tried before – either consciously or habitually – has failed, how do we know in which direction to take our first step? Start with a map.

THE FIRST MAP: RESPONSIBILITY

"The best day of your life is the one on which you decide your life is your own. No apologies or excuses. No one to lean on, rely on, or blame. The gift is yours - it is an amazing journey - and you alone are responsible for the quality of it. This is the day your life really begins."

— Bob Moawad

1

The Responsibility Pendulum

The goal of this map is to show you what you are responsible for and what you are not responsible for, because happiness comes from taking on just the right amount of responsibility. Not too little, not too much, but *just enough.*

I've put together a lot of words in an attempt to explain or convince you of the truth of that statement - and to help you create the right balance in your own life - but the premise is ultimately just that simple. If you want to be happy, you have to figure out what you are responsible for and what you are not. More specifically, you need to take ownership of your own thoughts, feelings and actions while letting go of the responsibility for the thoughts, feelings and actions of others.

You're the boss of you, and no one else.

It sounds obvious, and yet it seems that the majority of us suffer from some kind of emotional distress, relationship woes, or all around dissatisfaction with life because we struggle to get that balance right.

Too Much

The list of things for which I have held myself accountable is long. I am responsible for whether or not I am happy or sad. I am responsible for whether or not my work gets done. I have *also* taken responsibility for whether or not my husband is happy, what kind of people my children grow up to be, whether my friends feel valued and appreciated, whether or not my mother knows that she's a good mom, how successful my siblings are, and whether or not Palestine and Israel ever get their acts together.

OK, fine. Maybe peace in the Middle East is a stretch, but it is perfectly reasonable to assume that I am responsible for how my husband, Jared, is feeling at every minute of every day, right? If he's feeling happy or proud or secure, it is because I am a good wife. If he's feeling sad, angry, frustrated, or insecure, on the other hand, it is a sign that I have failed and am, therefore, not a good enough wife. Ergo, his happiness is my responsibility.

Likewise, it is my job as a parent to make sure that my children are happy and that they turn out to be good people. If they are ever sad, rude, scared, frustrated, irresponsible, or loud in public, it is a reflection of my failure to do my job. And, like most mothers, I will do absolutely everything in my power to avoid failing, because to do so would mean, in a nutshell, that I suck.

The list of self-imposed responsibilities continues. When family comes to visit, it is my job to ensure they enjoy every moment of their vacation. They are to sleep well, eat well, and fall madly in love with the city in which I live. They are never to experience boredom or feel that their presence has caused me anything but bliss. When I come to visit them, however, they should never be stressed out from trying to accommodate me. Everyone I care about, in other words, should always be at peace, especially when they interact with me.

That might all sound a little crazy when it's in black and white, but most people with kids would admit that we tend to feel proud when our children succeed and disappointed in ourselves when they fail. We can't take ownership of one without inheriting responsibility for the other. Similarly, a lot of people in relationships feel guilty if their partners are unhappy. Crazy or not, many of us have taken on responsibility for our loved ones' happiness.

Here's the problem: no matter what I do, I cannot control how other people feel. I can't make someone enjoy their vacation, love broccoli, look forward to homework, or appreciate the romance of musical-night-in. Also, people big and small make their own decisions, and those decisions have consequences. Trying to be responsible for that which we can't control is bound to make us unhappy. We get angry, frustrated, and anxious as we watch our best attempts fail. We're mad at ourselves for failing and mad at our loved ones for not following instructions. This is inevitable; there is no way to avoid failure when you attempt to take responsibility for someone else's life.

Too Little

At the other extreme, we have times when we do not take enough responsibility for our own feelings, thoughts, or actions. As eager as we can be to take charge of everyone else's actions, we are just as quick to believe it is not our responsibility or *our fault* if we are happy, sad, or mad.

It is not my fault my job sucks (because my boss is a jerk).

It's not my fault that I can't lose weight (because my husband keeps bringing home junk food).

It's not my fault that I'm angry (because the world is full

of morons).

This is what the self-help world calls "the victim mentality." You are a victim of your circumstances; you are at the mercy of everyone you encounter. It is, as the word "victim" suggests, a position without power. When you give the responsibility for your feelings, thoughts or actions to someone else, you give away your power. Your power to choose. Your power to change. Your power to be happy.

Tragically, you are giving that power to someone who is destined to fail. Just as you can't succeed at making others happy, there is no way that someone else can make you happy or unhappy, no matter how much you insist that it is their job *or* their fault. Only you can decide what goes on in your own head and heart.

Just Right

The path to happiness lies somewhere in between these two extremes. On that path, you can accept responsibility for your own feelings, thoughts and actions while allowing others to hold on to that same power for themselves. There, you can be compassionate without being accountable for someone else's pain. You can acknowledge consequences without assigning blame. On this middle ground, you are able to support others without losing your ability to stand on your own two feet.

The fact that you are responsible for your own happiness should be good news; you have all the control here! And yet, it's a truth that I am always hesitant to tell, especially to unhappy people. It's not easy to hear that we are to blame, mostly, for our own misery.

But there *is* good news.

If you are the boss of your own unhappiness, then you are also the boss of your own happiness.

And you're basically the world's best boss.

Coming Back To Center

I call this balancing act the Responsibility Pendulum, which reminds me that most of us swing back and forth between extremes.

I used to assume that I was nobly taking on too much responsibility at all times, but I learned that I was also placing much of the burden of my happiness on other people's shoulders. While I was busy making sure my husband was feeling loved, he was supposed to be taking care of my need to feel special. While I made sure my kids felt secure, they were supposed to be making me feel appreciated. Even now, after lots of therapy, hours of research, and thousands of words written about personal responsibility, I still find myself getting off kilter from time to time and looking to others to make me feel loved, valued, or good enough. When that happens, there is one question I use to help bring me back to center:

"What did I do to get here?"

Asking this reminds me that I am not only responsible for my current circumstances, but that I have the power to change them. That mental switch from blaming to accountability is often uncomfortable at first, especially when the answer is "something stupid." But, I ultimately feel more in control of my life. I'm reminded of my power to make new choices, ones that may fix mistakes I've made or simply help me move on to the next thing. Bringing the focus back to me also forces to me to let go of the reins on other people's stuff because it ensures my hands are full of my own crap. Embracing temporary tunnel vision for my own thoughts, feelings, and actions lets everyone else off the hook for fixing me and relieves them from the nightmare of having me try to fix them.

You can bring yourself back to center by acknowledging the choices you made that brought you to this moment. "What did I do to get here?" Take inventory. Don't worry about assigning judgment or justifying why you made the choices you did; just admit and accept that the present is a natural consequence of your past decisions. You were the boss then, and you're the boss now. The sooner you can claim ownership of what was, the sooner you can move on to what is and what will be.

No one is better suited to take control and turn things around than you are. No one has the same access to your innermost desires, which puts you in the perfect position to see those desires become reality. You also have the inside track on what pisses you off, what scares you, what situations to avoid, and what hot buttons need to be accounted for. No one knows you like you do.

In other words, you've got this.

2

The Symbiotic Relationship

We are each responsible for securing our own happiness. It sounds obvious and even trite. So why is something so seemingly simple so apparently difficult in real life?

I blame my mother.

I called her one day to share with her a breakthrough my husband and I had experienced in a marriage counseling session.

"I always assumed that, in a perfect marriage, I would dedicate myself to making him happy." I told her. "At the same time, he would dedicate himself to making me happy, and the end result would be that we would both be making each other happy."

"Right – exactly!" my mother chimed in.

"No, actually. That's *exactly* wrong," I said. "That is what's known as a symbiotic relationship, which is the same kind of relationship that our bodies have with intestinal bacteria. We try to sustain each other instead of taking care of ourselves."

"Well, that sounds very romantic to me," she said.

"And now I understand why I ended up in marriage counseling."

In my mom's defense, the idea of finding someone to make you happy instead of learning how to make yourself happy is pervasive. It's the underlying theme of every romance story ever told. Books, movies, and TV shows are filled with examples of people finally finding happiness in others – sometimes happiness so new they didn't even know they wanted it. In defense of the storyteller, we are taught in junior high English to show rather than tell, and inner growth and personal responsibility isn't easy to show. But in real life, it's the internal heroics we never see that often determine whether an ending is happy or tragic.

What Is A Symbiotic Relationship?

The term symbiosis comes from biology, and it describes when two organisms work together as one to achieve a mutually beneficial goal. The relationship goes beyond simple cooperation; the two organisms need each other to survive. As long as everyone is doing their job, it sounds like a good thing, and it is when you're talking about plants that grow on rocks or bacteria that live inside intestinal tubing. It is less appealing and efficient in terms of human relationships.

Symbiotic relationships occur between people when both parties attempt to make the other happy or healthy. That still doesn't sound so bad, and it can even be natural in the beginning of a relationship. As Jennifer Pattison, a Certified Imago Relationship Therapist, explains, "In the romantic love stage this seems easy because we are fueled with hormones that make us feel euphoric. It takes less effort by our partner to make us feel happy and we are extra motivated to go out of our comfort zone to make our partner happy. Once those hormones wear off we enter a power struggle, with each of us trying to get our partner to meet our needs (make us happy)." That's where the trouble starts.

Because it is impossible to make someone else happy - what with our lack of mind reading abilities and our unique sets of wants and needs - we're pretty much guaranteed to fail in this well-intentioned endeavor. And when we do, we end up feeling frustrated, unloved, neglected, angry, abused, and taken for granted. We try to push our partners into being more like us so that they'll be easier to please and better able to predict what we need. We resent each other for not trying hard enough. We insist that we have grown apart, and point to our inability to know how to please each other as proof.

Relationship experts often describe this as a codependent relationship, and everyone loses. You'll each suffer the double whammy of feeling like a failure for not being able to make your partner happy and being unhappy yourself because your partner is incapable of meeting all your needs. Jennifer says, "If you tell yourself your partner is responsible for your unhappiness then you are probably in a codependent relationship."

Becoming Two Wholes

Untangling yourself from a symbiotic relationship can be messy. It feels like a horrible game of trust and chance, where both parties carefully count down to the moment of letting go and hope that you both know you're going *on* three and not *after* three. You both have to let go of each other and pick yourselves back up, and there's a natural fear that someone is going to get dropped in the process. You might also have to actively challenge most of what you've been taught about what makes someone a good partner.

I've always believed that a good woman - and especially a good mother and wife - was a happy saint, who not only gives, but gives to the detriment of her own needs. A good woman never worries about herself, never complains, and never asks for anything from anyone.

A good woman is a martyr, basically.

With all due respect to the martyrs, I think it's important to point out that *their stories do not end well.* They die and become symbols for all the people who were not burned at the stake. I mean, it sounds very admirable in theory, but the reality is pretty damn bleak. And still that ideal persists among women everywhere.

My goal is not martyrdom or sainthood. I just want a happy, healthy relationship with my husband. Sometimes that means taking care of myself.

I remember once when I decided to spend a day shopping alone because Jared was in a bad mood. I'd asked him a few times what was wrong, and he repeatedly insisted he was fine. As I gathered up my purse and shopping list, I looked at him and said, "I'm in a good mood today. I really don't want you to spoil that, so I'm going to go shopping on my own. I hope you figure out what's up and are more pleasant to be around when I get home." He looked a little shell-shocked as I gave him a kiss and walked out the door.

Despite my outward confidence, I was worried that I was being a bad wife. I wondered if I should have tried harder to get him to talk to me, or stayed home to make him feel better. Maybe I would have made him more comfortable if I'd pretended everything was fine. But we'd agreed by that point that we would each be responsible for our own happiness, so I left him with his sour mood and went off to do my own thing. When I got home a few hours later, I found a chipper husband who'd apparently worked through whatever had been bugging him - without any help from me.

Of course, that doesn't mean that people in a healthy relationship can't help one another. In fact, asking for help and learning to rely on each other can build incredible intimacy. It's not a bad thing to lean on each other or ask for help. The key, however, is to remember who is ultimately responsible for those needs, and who is pitching in to help out of love. There's a phrase I use to help me maintain that balance:

"This is what I need right now, and I'd like to be able to get it from you."

These words remind me that I'm responsible for knowing what I need and asking for it. It also lets Jared know that he can step in and help, but that I'm ultimately in charge of making sure those needs are met. What's not said, but implied, is that Jared can also choose to say no, and it will be my job to find another solution.

It requires a huge amount of trust and vulnerability to put your needs out there and accept that the person you love most could deny your request. Working up the nerve to ask for help around the house can be challenging, and it's downright humiliating to say, "I'm feeling really insecure right now and I'd really appreciate it if you'd tell me that I'm pretty." Making these requests doesn't just expose our needs, it lays bare our weaknesses and the holes we're hoping to have filled by our loved one. There's no doubt that this kind of vulnerability is scary, but it's also an opportunity to experience real intimacy and connection with your partner.

The good news is that someone who loves you is likely to want to contribute to your happiness in any way they can. There have been very few times when Jared or I have responded to an honest, clear request with, "Well, I'm sorry, but I can't do that. Good luck!" Remembering that takes the edge off of asking just a little bit. And when someone willingly, without guilt or coercion, gives of him- or herself in response to your call for help, you feel loved and cherished.

3

When Helping Hurts

Taking responsibility for your own thoughts, feelings, and actions is only half of the equation. To be truly happy, you must also learn how to stop taking responsibility for other people's thoughts, feelings, actions, and happiness. For me, this is the hard part. I've found it is much easier to take responsibility for my own happiness than it is to let other people enjoy that same right.

I'm really good at taking care of everyone else. Because I obviously have all the answers to life, I'm eager to *help* other people live theirs better. Unfortunately, few people are eager to have anyone - even someone as enlightened and flawless as me - tell them how they can be fixed.

Sarcasm aside, it can be a struggle to stop helping people. Helping, after all, is a good thing. I was raised with a collection of mantras that espoused the importance of taking care of other people.

It takes a village.

I am my brother's keeper.

No man is an island.

I don't subscribe to the belief that this is a dog-eat-dog world. Furthermore, research has shown that doing good things for other people can increase your own happiness. How, then, can helping interfere with happiness? To understand this apparent paradox, we have to look closer at the nuances of helping.

Unsolicited Help

In our house, we have two rules about helping:

1. We only give help when it is asked for.
2. We help those who first try to help themselves.

The inception of these rules was motivated by my desire to prevent my oldest child from being bossy and my youngest child from being whiny.

My son, Devin, has a talent for recognizing when things aren't being done right. He can often tell a sentence is going to end incorrectly even before the speaker has a chance to finish it. His sister is usually the beneficiary of these gifts. He is quick to jump in and tell her how to do her chores right, how to fix her homework, and how she could get ready faster in the morning. When she snaps at him to leave her alone, he insists that he is "trying to help."

"We only give help when it's asked for," I remind him. "It's not really helping if she doesn't want your help. It feels more like being picked on."

This pattern plays out among adults, too. We offer to help and then we are surprised and resentful when our friends and family don't appreciate our efforts. The problem is that unsolicited help can feel more like judgment, and most of us respond to judgment with resentment. If a friend is constantly telling us that our boyfriend is a jerk, we're more likely to avoid the friend than ditch the boyfriend. When our mother-in-law offers her best child-rearing advice, we complain to our husbands because his mother obviously hates us. Likewise, when we give budget tips to our shopping-crazed girlfriends, they're probably going to make no changes to their financial habits and simply stop inviting us to the mall.

Why are well-meaning attempts to help so often misinterpreted at judgment? We miss the mark, in part, because we don't really know what we're aiming for. If we haven't been directly asked for help, then what we're doing is making assumptions about what we think is needed. We have to use our own experience and perceptions to fill in the gaps, and our solutions are little more than wild guesses, shots in the dark that are more likely to wound than fix.

I see this happen a lot when people try to help the poor. Committees are formed and Facebook discussions are had to examine what's wrong with people today. Assumptions are made about someone's willingness to work or unwillingness to properly budget their money. From an ivory tower, judgments are handed down about bad choices people make and what good deeds will end the blight of poverty.

What I don't see nearly as frequently is an attempt to understand poverty from the perspective of the people who are living in it. People make assumptions based on what they see from their vantage points behind a cashier stand or a desk in the ER, but they don't sit beside the poor and ask why fake nails are easier to come by than health insurance or monthly groceries. Because we don't take the time to understand the problem, our efforts to help rarely succeed.

We make similarly misguided assumptions within our individual relationships.

I have a friend who asked her parents for money for Christmas one year. She said she had everything she needed, and what she really wanted was some breathing room in her monthly budget. Her parents, however, didn't want her to think they hadn't put any thought into her gift, so they gave her a gift certificate for a massage instead. "It's not that I don't appreciate the thought," my friend told me, "but I would have enjoyed knowing my gas bill was paid much more than an hour-long massage - and now I have to find childcare to use their gift."

When we aren't asked - or we choose to ignore exactly what was asked for - we have to fill in the blanks with our own assumptions. Occasionally we might guess right and wind up looking like the hero, but chances are better that we wind up feeling resentful because our efforts aren't appreciated.

I remember one night a few years ago when Jared and I were on our way to a restaurant, and I noticed that he was being unusually quiet. "What's wrong?" I asked.

"Nothing," he said.

A few more minutes of silence passed, and I tried again. "Jared, I know something is wrong. What's going on?"

"Nothing, jeez, what am I doing?"

"That's just it! You're not doing or saying anything, and now you're biting my head off."

"I'm just driving, Britt."

"How can I help you if you don't tell me what's wrong?"

"I'm not asking for your help, and you're making things worse by trying to push your help onto me!"

It stung to hear at the time, but he was right. Jared explained later that he likes to be able to have some time to think about things that are bothering him on his own before sharing them with me. As it turns out, my insistence that Jared talk to me doesn't make him feel better, but makes him feel guilty for not being able to put on a happy face.

I hate this. I think talking through your feelings is almost always a better alternative than stewing in them alone. But I don't get to make that call for anyone but me. Jared has the right to cope with his own emotions the way he sees best, and I have a responsibility to keep my help to myself.

Help Those Who Help Themselves

I have to admit that I'm still very uncomfortable with this phrase. I came up with it in response to my daughter's tendency to whine. It's easy to say, "I only help people who help themselves" when a seven year old is insisting you pick out her socks, or when she's lying in her bed demanding someone make her breakfast. But as much as I value self-sufficiency in my kids, I also don't want them to think I'm advocating turning a blind eye to the truly helpless.

I wouldn't pass by a sick person on the street because they couldn't verbalize their needs properly. Nor would I ignore the signs of a depressed or suicidal teen, waiting to step in until they could correctly tell me that something was wrong. There are definitely cases when an unrequested intervention is appropriate. However, these instances are exceptions to the rule.

When you're talking about relationships with able-bodied adults or capable children, it makes sense to reserve your assistance for those who not only ask for help, but who have made an attempt to help themselves. This demonstrates that they are invested in the outcome at least as much as you are, and hopefully more. After all, the person who cares the most will take on the lion's share of the responsibility.

This is a good rule to remember when someone tries to hand you responsibility for their happiness. You probably won't hear someone say, "here, you be in charge of my life, I'm not interested in helping myself," but you probably have heard other code phrases that essentially make the same offer.

"You make me mad." (You can also make me happy.)

"I was in a great mood until you said that." (You broke it, you fix it.)

"I just love you so much, I can't help that I'm jealous." (It's not my responsibility, so it must be yours.)

When confronted with these offers, it's up to you to decide whether or not to take the deal. You can lament that the unhappy people around you insist on making you responsible for their problems, or you can choose not to pick up their crap. Just because someone else isn't claiming ownership of his or her happiness doesn't mean you have to accept it. Let someone else pick it up, or let it sit long enough for the rightful owner to claim it. What happens to it isn't your responsibility.

It's About Trust

When Devin tells his little sister what to do, he isn't just helping her; he's helping Mom and Dad do their job. He doesn't always understand why we let her stumble through her chores or figure out the answers to her homework on her own. In his mind, he's stepping in because no one else will. We're quick to remind him that Emma already has parents. More importantly, we try to assure him that he can trust us to do our job, even if it looks to him like we're messing it up.

It's that same kind of trust that will let you leave others in charge of their own happiness. You have to trust that they know what happiness looks like for them. You have to trust that they'll find their own paths, in their own time. You have to trust that they possess everything they need to live the lives they're destined for. You have to trust them to ask for help if they need or want it. And you have to trust yourself to be able to handle whatever happens.

When I ask my husband what is wrong, it's not because I'm crazy. I ask about his well-being when he is giving off signs that something is bothering him. He may be quieter than normal, short tempered, or just acting differently in small, almost imperceptible ways that only someone close to him would notice. In other words, when he tells me "nothing" is wrong, I can usually tell if that's true or not. He has agreed to try and tell me when "nothing" means "nothing I want to talk about right now," so that I don't make up all sorts of stories in my head about how I am to blame for his obvious unhappiness, but he doesn't always remember to do that. "Nothing I want to talk about" is still not easy for me to hear, but I've learned that I have to trust him to be in charge of his own emotions.

I've also had to trust him to find his own unique definition of and path to happiness, something that is especially difficult for me because of my interest in personal development. I spent years leaving books on his nightstand, emailing him links to articles, and practicing pop psychology on long car rides. He never showed any interest in the resources I shared, and I've had to accept he never might. A few years ago, however, he experienced his own awakening - with no help from me.

I had read about Body for Life, a 12-week diet and exercise program that involved daily workouts and careful tracking of meals. Jared had been talking for ages about getting into better shape, but hadn't ever taken any action. He suggested we do the 3-month program together. I agreed, and waited for him to get a copy of the workbook.

After several weeks of waiting, I set a start date for myself, and joined the YMCA by our house. The night before my first workout, I sat at our kitchen counter with my workbook and planned the exercises I'd be doing in the morning.

"I thought we were going to do this together?" Jared said when he saw me filling out my meal plan and studying the exercise diagrams.

"I thought so too, but you never got around to getting your stuff. I told you this was my start date, and I'm not waiting for you anymore. I'm doing this for me."

A week later, Jared sat at the kitchen counter and planned the next day's workout in his own planner. I hadn't said another word about his goals or us working together; it seemed he'd decided on his own it was finally time to act. For the next 12 weeks, Jared worked hard in the gym and followed his meal plans carefully. I did the same, and we swapped war stories, but we rarely worked out together or did our planning at the same time. We each completed our own three-month challenge, and it was the first time I remembered seeing Jared follow through on a commitment like that without any interference from me.

During that three-month time, Jared and I also quit smoking. Jared made his own doctor's appointment to get a prescription for Chantix. He also started using a day planner and completing long-neglected projects around the house. He began to send me links to articles about health and happiness - some of which I'd already sent him but he'd only read when he'd discovered them himself.

I remember these accomplishments - and all of the things Jared does daily without my involvement - when he tells me that nothing is wrong. I remember them when he seems sad and insists I can't help. It might be obvious to other people, but it's not always easy for me to remember to trust my husband to take care of his own happiness.

It can also be hard to trust our friends to know what's best for themselves, especially when all evidence suggest that they are currently floundering. The reality, I tell myself, is that we all flounder from time to time, but my friends are just as capable of recovering as I have been. Like me, they possess everything they need to be happy. Whether or not they use the tools they have - and when - is up to them.

4

When Happiness Is Hard

Gurus have been telling us for decades that we choose what our lives look like. In reality, however, it's a little more complicated than that. In the real world, we don't always get to choose between being miserable or being blissed out of our minds. Sometimes the choice we have to make is between shitty and less shitty.

I used to insist that I couldn't get on a regular sleep schedule because my husband is a night owl. I am a morning person by nature, but I felt bad going to bed early when Jared wanted to stay up late and watch TV together. "I can't keep doing this," I'd tell him when I struggled to get up with my alarm the morning after a midnight sitcom marathon.

I wanted Jared to go to bed with me at about 9:30 every night. We'd have time to talk, snuggle, and maybe even read quietly before drifting off to sleep. I'd get a good eight hours of sleep and still be able to wake up at 6 AM, a full hour before the kids had to be up. Unfortunately, Jared had no interest in this regimen.

After 13 years of sharing a bed, I finally figured out that I had to choose between staying up late to spend quality time with my husband or waking up early each morning to get stuff done. I could not, however, have both.

I decided that feeling rested was crucial to my well-being and productivity. I took a few cues from Dr. Google and developed a nighttime routine that ended with me quietly reading in bed for about 20 minutes. I even asked Jared not to bring the iPad into the bedroom after I got into bed. Now, most nights I go to bed alone, but I almost never find myself accidentally sleeping until noon on a workday.

That's not to say that going to bed without my husband was the right choice. I could have just as easily decided to enjoy those precious couple of hours with Jared late at night, and I would have been just as "right." Making choices about our lives is rarely about picking between right and wrong. It's usually about making the best choice we can and, most importantly, taking responsibility for the consequences of that choice.

It's OK To Hate The Choice

Although we always have choices to make that can move us towards or away from happiness, there's no denying that we are often handed tough choices by other people.

Addicts are notorious for giving their loved ones the choice between bad and worse. Stay in the hell you're familiar with, or leave for an unknown that doesn't include the people you love the most. A woman who spent a decade married to an alcoholic once told me that she felt like she was constantly choosing between two losing scenarios when it came to her husband's inability to be responsible with money. "I could just pick up the slack myself and feel resentful, or I could fight about it constantly and feel like shit every day."

Of course, we have the choice to walk away from

irresponsible people, but that's not always an easy or even happy alternative. A man whose wife had an affair once told me that he was most angry with her for saddling him with two awful options. "Either I leave and have to live without her, or I stay and become the pathetic man who stayed with the woman who cheated on him." Although the choice was his to make, neither forgiveness nor divorce were easy options.

You might have to choose between staying in a job where the boss is a jerk or facing the uncertainty of unemployment.

Do you choose to constantly argue with your adult child over his refusal to pay his student loans, or do you maintain your relationship while struggling financially to pay back loans for which you'd co-signed?

It's your choice, the experts will tell you. And yes, it is, but it's OK to take a moment and be pissed off that someone else's poor behavior has left you with an awful decision. The next step, however, has to be asking yourself what you did to contribute to your present situation and what you can do next. When you ask and begin to answer that question, you'll break the cycle of blame and start to become aware of your own power.

Happiness And Tragedy

Some of the most difficult obstacles we have to overcome are really no one's fault. And then what?

What are we supposed to do when illness, death, betrayal, disaster, bad luck, and the innumerable other unhappy-making life things arrive on our doorstep? Are we to blame for not being happy when the really bad stuff happens?

No... but also, yes.

Natural disasters cannot be blamed on any one human (despite what Westboro Baptists might say). Losing your home to a fire, your job to lay-offs, or your loved one to illness are all very bad things for which you should accept no responsibility. It's just as unproductive to look for someone else to blame. These things happen, they suck, and there is little to be gained by trying to figure out why.

Neither is it productive to try and choose how we feel when the world falls down around our ears. You should never attempt to blithely "feel" happy in spite of pain. When tragedy or disaster strikes – and it will – it is natural and healthy to feel sad or angry. These feelings, these temporary responses to nasty situations, cannot be controlled. In fact, none of our feelings can be controlled; the only thing to do with feelings is to feel them.

But we can also remember that grief, fear, and disappointment can dance with happiness. It may be a slow, sad waltz, but it's still a beautiful dance to behold. I know because I've seen it.

My friend Lisa Gift-Kelly survived cancer twice before it returned with a vengeance a third time. After several months of treatment, it was obvious that she was not going to win this final battle, and she made the decision to stop the medications and painful procedures that were destroying her already fragile quality of life.

Lisa knew she was going to die. She knew she wasn't going to see her two daughters graduate from high school or grow old with her husband. And yet, she chose to spend the last year of her life embracing happiness wherever she could find it. She went to Disney World with her family and, on her last Mother's Day, took them to see the ocean. It was there that she helped my own daughter overcome her fear of the waves, and where she taught me the meaning of her favorite expression: It is what it is.

What it was for Lisa was laughing at inappropriate jokes,

loving her girls and her husband, and living as much as she could for as long as she could. Lisa chose happiness in the face of unavoidable death and devastating goodbyes. When she died at her home, surrounded by her family, it was absolutely heartbreaking for everyone who knew her and tragic for her husband and kids, but she had ensured that her story would be much more than a sad ending.

Rachel and Roger Reynolds made a similar choice. Their daughter, Charlotte, died of a brain tumor when she was just four years old. While they were obviously crushed by her death, they both continued to get up most mornings and put one foot in front of the other. They even found ways to channel their grief into projects that would help others. Rachel wrote a book, *Four Seasons for Charlotte*, which offers other parents insight into how to cope with childhood cancer. She and Roger also started CJ's Thumbs Up Foundation, a non-profit organization that provides financial support for the families of children with life-threatening illnesses.

About 18 months after Charlotte's death, Rachel and Roger opened up their home to me and my family, offering us a pit stop on our year-long road trip around America. I was in awe of their hospitality, kindness, and overall positivity, especially towards my daughter who was not much older than their own would have been. They smiled, laughed, fed my family, and were two of the warmest people you could ever meet. You'd never know that every day they face a life they never expected to have to endure when their little girl was born. You'd never know they're managing to choose happiness while living with eternal grief.

All around us are stories like these, stories of people who choose happiness even as life is handing them buckets of crap and unfairness. It sounds trite. It seems too simple. But it is, I'm convinced, absolutely true:

Happiness is always an option.

It's just not always *easy*.

Suggested Next Steps

As you work towards happiness using the map of Responsibility, consider taking some of these steps in your daily life:

- Ask yourself, "What did I do to get here?" Make a list of your answers. Acknowledge, accept, and prepare to move on.

- Practice asking for help clearly and calmly instead of expecting someone else to know what you need.

- Practice waiting to be asked for help before jumping in to fix, soothe, or solve a problem.

- Ask yourself, "what are the choices I can make right now?" Make a list of your options, even the sucky ones.

- Say no when you feel like saying no.

- Go on a gossip hiatus. This will help you see how much power you have over your own mood and environment.

Looking for more action steps? Every week I share a new happiness challenge online. These tiny assignments are based on science, research, and experience. Check out the latest challenge at http://inpursuitofhappiness.net/weekly-challenge/.

Map Notes

Map Notes

THE SECOND MAP: GROWTH

"If you want to get more out of life, you must lose your inclination for monotonous security and adopt a helter-skelter style of life that will at first appear to you to be crazy. But once you become accustomed to such a life you will see its full meaning and its incredible beauty."

— Jon Krakauer, *Into the Wild*

"The first kiss and the first glass of wine are the best."

— Marty Rubin

5

Novelty, Change, Growth

Anyone who has engaged in retail therapy can attest to the power of a new pair of shoes to create instant euphoria. Scientists have been able to attribute that rush of good vibes to a hormone spike in the brain that's trigged by exposure to something new. This is more than a little thrill; the chemical reactions to scoring a new handbag aren't all that different from the response an addict's brain might have to a dose of cocaine. Novelty is a powerful force, and this map is designed to show you how to channel that force into sustainable happiness.

Sustainability is the tricky part. Those little novelty jolts only provide short-term happiness. What is new today will be old tomorrow, and old doesn't seem to excite the brain in the same way.

We are naturally attracted to happiness, however, and so we seek out ways to feel that rush again once it's passed. We head back to the mall, or the dealer. We buy a bigger house, a newer car, and nicer clothes. But because the new will always and inevitably become old, we can never be satisfied.

This cycle of wanting, having, enjoying, getting bored,

and wanting more is known as the hedonic treadmill. It's a result of the brain's amazing ability to adapt combined with an innate need to feel joy. The hedonic treadmill is fueled by novelty, but that doesn't mean all novelty is bad.

The Myth Of Too Much Novelty

When I started my blog about happiness in 2010, I received several concerned emails about the name, In Pursuit of Happiness. I was warned repeatedly about the dangers of always chasing and never just accepting and being happy with what you have. While science and personal experience told me that novelty was an essential element of happiness, common sense suggested that there had to be a limit. How can we be happy if we can't be satisfied with old, when that is where everything is heading?

I turned to Google to help me understand the dangers of too much newness. I thought I would unearth a study or an expert that would tell me exactly where to find the line between happiness and unfulfilled obsession. Surprisingly, I couldn't come up with anything to support the idea that there is such a thing as too much personal growth or too much newness in a person's life. What I found instead was page after page of advice on how to inject the spark of novelty into stagnant relationships and boring lives.

Relationships notoriously get stale. Research has proven repeatedly that new love wears off and the honeymoon period does, in fact, end. As we adapt to one another, a love that was once passionate and exciting becomes comfortable and less intense. The thrill hormones in our brains slow, as does our pulse when we look at our too-familiar partner. And what, when the love wears off, do relationship experts recommend that we do?

In most cases, we are not told to find ourselves a new

partner. Nor are we told to just deal with the fact that long-term monogamy is boring. (If you have a counselor who tells you that, fire him.) No, relationship experts advise us to make the old new again.

Couples who find themselves in a lackluster rut are encouraged to learn a new skill together, to shake up their routines, and to make an effort to discover unfamiliar things about each other. They aren't warned about the danger of having a relationship that is too stimulating. They may, however, be counseled to simultaneously work on accepting their partner for who he or she is. Acceptance and novelty, in other words, are not mutually exclusive.

We have to accept that we always must be seeking happiness in some way.

Extrinsic Vs. Intrinsic Novelty

In the documentary film *Happy*, Professor Tim Kasser makes the distinction between intrinsic and extrinsic goals. Extrinsic goals are focused on external rewards, such as money, image, and status. Intrinsic goals, on the other hand, are based on values like personal growth, relationship, and a sense of community - ideas that are felt more than seen. According to Kasser, people focused on intrinsic goals are more like to be happy and less likely to feel stressed or anxious, while those who pursue extrinsic goals often report feeling dissatisfied with their life. Here, I think, lies the key to being able to experience the happiness of novelty without getting stuck on the hedonic treadmill.

If we want to seek long-lasting happiness, it's best to focus on sustainable - and intrinsic - newness. Sustainable newness affects who we are internally instead of just changing our surfaces. It includes things like discovering something new about our lover or learning a new skill. These fresh experiences provide longer-lasting happiness and are easier to come by than more money.

Having Vs. Doing

While you might often think of newness in terms of a thing you can acquire, it's good to remember that experiencing something for the first time is also a form of novelty. Think about your first day at a new job or your first night in a new apartment. Your senses were forced to come alive as you took in unfamiliar surroundings and tried to navigate foreign territory. That heightened awareness injects every moment of a new experience with a sense of adventure. Adventure, while potentially scary, is also a powerful catalyst for happiness.

I think this is why so many people love to travel. When you're visiting a new place, everything is novel. From the airport bathroom to the view out the hotel window, fresh input floods the senses and lights up the brain. This exhilaration caused by the unfamiliar is why tourists flock to a remote small town that residents would swear has nothing to offer. Of course in time, as the locals remind us, even the most fascinating place can become familiar and therefore dull.

Travel is really no more permanent a solution to happiness than a trip to the mall. You'll likely grow tired of an outfit before you run out of things to discover about a new metropolis, but all external changes – even a change in scenery - eventually lose their luster.

Change Vs. Growth

Change you seek as an escape can cause more harm than happiness. I've had many novel experiences that only pleased me for a short time before they left me depleted and desperate for more, and each time I can trace my attempts back to a need to be different than what I was.

I tried to completely reinvent myself during my freshman year of college. I chopped off my long, curly hair and bleached it (an act made more ridiculous by the fact that I have naturally blond hair). I pierced my belly button and then my tongue, got new tattoos, and tried desperately to become a punk rock rebel who was more cool than insecure. There's nothing inherently wrong with the bad-ass look, but none of those changes actually made me happier - nor did blogging to escape my marital problems, shopping to cover up my money worries, or moving to a new state to compensate for being unsure of who I was. That's not to say that I didn't learn anything from blogging, enjoy my new shoes, or stumble upon incredible opportunities after moving to Florida. But simply introducing something new into my life wasn't enough to fundamentally change me or make me happier on a long-term basis.

Growth is an entirely different type of change, one that is rooted in acceptance of who you are and where you are in your life. A carrot seed will grow into a carrot plant; no amount of fertilization will cause it to grow into an oak tree. Likewise, no amount of personal growth will fundamentally change who you are. It does, however, offer a constantly changing experience with the world.

As you grow, you interact with the world differently. Imagine that you came to the United States speaking no English. You then attended classes and learned to speak the language that you heard and saw all around you. As your knowledge of the language grew, your experience within the country would change. You'd be able to understand messages that were lost on you before, and you'd be able to contribute to your environment in different ways. Every new word learned would offer another opportunity for you to experience the thrill of novelty.

Personal growth is the internal change that allows you to interact with the world in new ways. You encourage it by challenging your perceptions, experimenting with your habits, and expanding your horizons.

6

Creating An Atmosphere Of Growth

Growth is a term that can make some people squeamish, especially if it's combined with the word "personal". Personal growth has a reputation for being more airy-fairy than useful, and more internal than tangible. But personal growth, just like plant growth or kid growth or any other kind of growth, is very real. It can be seen and, most importantly, cultivated.

Personal growth really just means adapting and learning. An atmosphere of growth, then, is one in which you are constantly learning.

Commit to learning, saying yes, and experimenting. Do new things. Plant something. Make something. Take a class. Try sushi. Read books about amoebas and architecture. Learn how to brew your own beer. Take pictures, and then learn how to take better ones. Read the manual to your sewing machine. Open your eyes to all that you don't know, and you will realize that you'll never run out of fuel for your happiness.

When you decide to seek out and accept new opportunities,

you'll be surprised how many present themselves to you. Oprah would say it's because you're attracting what you need, but it may just be that you're simply paying more attention. Whatever. Look for chances to grow, and you'll never be disappointed.

Break The Routine

If novelty is the catalyst for happiness, then routine is the mother of despair - or at least boredom. While your routines can provide stability and security in times of chaos, they also allow you to move through your days without thinking. Parts of your brain can shut down when you are running through your daily routines on autopilot. The most common example of this is the commute home that you don't remember taking because your brain determines the uneventful trip is unworthy of recording permanently.

How much of your life are you subconsciously deciding isn't worth remembering? What the hell is the point of all that unremarkable time?

It stands to reason that a brain on autopilot is not feeling happy, and that a life unremembered is not enjoyed. It also makes sense, then, that an easy way to wake yourself up from this lull is to break your routines.

The break doesn't have to be dramatic. Brush your teeth with your non-dominant hand one morning. Take a new route to work. Reach into the back of your closet and wear that shirt you forgot you had. Cook something new for dinner, or eat on a picnic blanket instead of at the table.

The act itself doesn't have to be something joyous - even the most optimistic person would struggle to get jazzed about oral hygiene and traffic patterns. But turning left when you usually turn right forces you to become more conscious, and you can only experience happiness when you're aware.

My husband once told me that he felt like he had been numb for several years. "I wasn't unhappy," he said, "but I wouldn't say I was happy either." He was just going through the motions. His wife kicking him out of the house shook up his routine a bit, and so did driving a motorcycle to work instead of a truck. A series of big and small changes, he said, woke him up. "I feel like I'm actually more aware of what's going on around me."

You have to be awake and aware before you can experience happiness.

Growth Makes Us Unhappy First

You should know going into this that growth is not always fun initially. Although the end result of this growth is happiness, the journey will take you through a period of discomfort and discouragement. Some sort of unhappiness is practically guaranteed to be a part of any personal growth spurt. You might hate growth before it makes you happy.

Doesn't that make you want to run right out and get started?

Happiness author Gretchen Rubin writes on her blog, "Novelty and challenge bring happiness. I believed that this observation was true for a lot of people, but I didn't think it would be true for *me*. I love routine. I revel in the little pleasures of my ordinary day. I don't like to travel. I don't even like to go to new restaurants. My favorite thing to do is to hang around the house and read in my pajamas." But in testing the theory for her book, *The Happiness Project*, Gretchen learned that even she would eventually succumb to the magic of growth, but not without first having to endure some growing pains.

"Novelty and challenge often mean delayed happiness. First comes a stressful period of feeling frustrated, stupid, exposed, insecure, confused...but along with that discomfort, you get a big surge of happiness. That's exactly what happened to me with my blog."

I decided at 32 years old to learn how to knit. Despite having no hand-eye coordination and being generally uncrafty, I wanted to be able to make my mom a scarf for Christmas. So, I bought a starter kit that included two sizes of needles and an instructional book. When that instructional booklet failed me completely, I turned to YouTube for guidance.

I spent the first several nights knitting, swearing, and unknitting.

Eventually, however, with more YouTube videos, a review of that booklet, and a hands-on lesson from a friend, I started to get it. Something clicked, and I transformed a ball of yarn into a beautiful infinity scarf that my mother could actually wear. True, much of my success hinged on the fact that a mother is easily impressed by things her children create, but I was elated. I continue to knit today and get a thrill every time I turn string into fabric.

I've followed this same pattern with nearly every domestic or crafty skill I've acquired. I've also sworn at computer screens while figuring out HTML and cried on a driving range when learning how to golf. While I never got past the unhappy stage with golf, most of my tear-soaked endeavors have ended with feelings of triumph, achievement, and happiness.

The idea of learning is exciting. The moment you realize you're finally getting it is empowering. But the actual process of learning is frustrating, demoralizing, and not at all what we would define as happiness. Still, this atmosphere of growth yields moments of happiness that outlast the agony of learning, and it is far more sustainable than a crack habit or shopping addiction.

Personal Growth Is The Most Uncomfortable

Learning to purl stitch was frustrating, but it doesn't hold a candle to the agony of adjusting to a new identity. Growth that results in a new label or a new image for ourselves - whether it's good or bad - is the hardest to accept.

Before Karen Walrond was a best-selling author, she was a lawyer. More than that, she was a female, African-American lawyer living and practicing in Texas. That specific mix of accomplishments is admirable. Impressive, even.

"And frankly," Karen told me, "it's kind of sexy when people say 'what do you do' to say 'I'm an attorney'." Karen admitted that even after she'd published *The Beauty of Different*, even when she was speaking professionally as a writer and photographer, she usually made sure to tell people she was a non-practicing attorney when they asked what she did. She even continued to pay her annual bar fees to ensure that she was still technically a lawyer. "That was the hardest thing to let go of. Who am I if I'm not an attorney?" Karen stopped practicing law in October of 2008, and she says it took her four years to get to the point where she no longer lead with her title as an attorney. "Now I tell people for accuracy's sake more than for ego."

I've held on to all kinds of labels and often struggled to make positive changes in my life for fear of the change it would require in my identity. Going from a homeowner to a full-time traveler and then to a renter was surprisingly difficult. The thought of no longer being a wife or a "happily married woman" kept me out of marriage counseling for years when it was obvious there were problems we needed to address. My fear of being "someone with depression" prevented me from seeing a doctor for months, and even the strangeness of calling myself "a writer" has gotten in the way of me pursuing my goals from time to time.

We cling to familiar versions of ourselves regardless of how good they are for us. A person who has always been obese may struggle to lose weight because they are committed to the idea of being "the fat guy." Quitting smoking is made more difficult by the thought of becoming a non-smoker, someone who may be perceived as being less cool than a smoker. When my mom earned her master's degree in Nursing at 51, she confessed to me that she was afraid she'd never be able to see herself as a professional, despite student loans and certifications to the contrary.

Dropping our labels means moving from a place of comfort, where we know who we are and how to interact with the world, to a place of uncertainty. Even if we assume the new version would be better, the fact that we don't know exactly what we're getting into makes us nervous. Actually, it usually scares the shit out of us, and we might not even realize that's what's keeping us from experiencing the change we crave.

The only way to overcome this discomfort and achieve significant growth is to stand with it. It helps to figure out exactly what identity we're clinging to and what values and stories we've attached to them. My mother, for example, realized that she equated being professional with being stiff and unapproachable, and she'd always prided herself on being accessible to her patients. She realized, however, that a professional image would instill a different kind of trust in people, one that would make her less likely to be hugged but better able to perform as a primary care provider. Getting to the root of our labels makes it a little easier to weather the uncertainty. And, when we can identify what we stand to gain by taking on new labels, it can be easier to let go of the old ones.

7

It's Never Too Late For Growth

Sometimes, we stop trying new things because we feel the time for new things has passed. We took other paths, we tell ourselves, and we just have to accept the choices we made and move on.

Or maybe we assume we are too grown up for starting over, and that surely it makes more sense to figure out how to just be happy with what we have, or at least with only the sensible new things. We should stick with gardening, or maybe sewing. We should throw ourselves into volunteering at our children's school or dedicate our free time to traveling more, because that's what people our age do.

We might think it's too late to try new things that call for reinvention, what with old dogs having such difficulty with new tricks.

We would be wrong.

I met Bill Rousseau at the City Market Art Center, a building in downtown Savannah filled with studio galleries where artists create and hawk their wares. My family was walking from shop to shop, marveling at the talent and weeping at the beauty we couldn't bring back to our RV-sized home. We found Bill upstairs in studio five, looking down his nose through his large glasses as he painted a layer of dense shrubbery in front of an old Savannah home. The one-room gallery in which he sat smelled of wet paint, and the walls and floors were covered with framed oil portraits of historic homes.

"Do we have budding artists here?" the white-haired man at the easel asked upon hearing my two children, Devin and Emma, comment on the various portraits and beg for one to take home.

"We do," I said.

The artist turned from his painting and leaned closer to Emma, who was obviously enthralled with the process. "Would you like to help me with this painting?" She nodded, and he handed her a brush tipped with fresh white paint. "Here," he pointed to an area – a shockingly *large* area – on his developing masterpiece and instructed Emma to make small white dots where she thought flowers should go.

I held my breath in anticipation - a mixture of pride, joy and fear beating in my chest as I watched my daughter, the budding artist, leave her mark on this man's work. When she finished, he thanked her and she grinned sheepishly. He turned to my son and asked if he, too, wanted to be an artist.

"I want to be a scientist," my pragmatic 11 year old replied.

"Oh, that's a very good thing," said the artist. "I was a scientist."

Devin's eyes lit up and my instincts buzzed. *An artist scientist?*

A few minutes later, we were leaving the gallery when my

gut tugged at me. "I, uh, I need to go back," I told Jared. "I'll catch up to you guys." Devin, my budding scientist, followed me back.

I cautiously stepped into the studio, apprehensive about intruding on the artist's space, time and life story. "Excuse me, I'm sorry to bother you, but, uh..." how do you explain that you're kind of obsessed with ordinary people who do extraordinary things? "I'm, uh, I'm a writer." That always seems to be a good opening. After a little more stumbling and questioning on my part, the artist scientist began to tell me his story.

Bill began his career as a scientist working in engineering and applied math. He didn't hate it and wasn't mediocre, which you might expect upon hearing that he's since become a painter. In fact, he was very good at being a scientist and engineer. He was the Director of Technologies for United Technologies, which equates to being a very big deal in the field.

"I had a very good career," Bill said with a smile and not an ounce of resentment or regret.

And then, at 55, he retired and enrolled in art school.

In 2002, he and his wife moved from Syracuse, New York to Savannah, Georgia where Bill could enroll in the Savannah College of Art and Design (SCAD). Bill had always enjoyed painting and figured it was time to do what he loved.

"Why would you go to school?" I asked. "Why not just paint if that's what you liked to do?"

"I didn't think I was good enough yet."

Bill wanted to paint in the style of the old masters and SCAD, he said, has a very good program for teaching that style. He admitted that his former career had allowed him and his wife to save enough money to support the move and change in lifestyle. And yet, as I spoke with him, he was sitting in front of a portrait that would hopefully be sold for several hundred dollars in a gallery that requires rent and utilities and financial support.

"Why not just paint?" I asked again. "I mean, why turn it into a business?"

"I like meeting people and talking to people, but mostly I love the idea of someone else loving my work and hanging it in their home. The idea of my paintings being in someone's home is a real thrill for me."

We chatted a little more and then I thanked Bill for his time and went on to catch up with my family. Later that day, while we combed the shelves of a local art supply store for acrylic paint and canvas pads for the kids, I heard Devin marvel aloud at what he'd heard back in the art gallery.

"Man, he's done everything I love. Science, math, *and* art. I didn't know you could do *all* those things!"

"Baby, you can do whatever you want," I told him. "And remember that you don't have to do *anything* forever. It's never too late to change your mind and do something different."

He nodded and picked out a paint brush.

I remember Bill sometimes when I think about all of the things I didn't do when I was younger. I didn't graduate from college because I had a baby, got married, and started working to support my new family. I didn't move to New York when I was young and reckless enough to possibly make a go of it. I didn't travel abroad during our year of nomadic living, and now I've promised my son that he can stay in one city until he graduates high school.

It's tempting to tell myself that there are dreams for which it is too late to try. What's the point of going to law school in your thirties? And it'd probably be too hard to learn a new language now. But Bill the artist-scientist reminds me that it is never too late. It's never too late to try something new, to start over, or to begin a brand new adventure.

Barbara Weibel started her own new adventure at the age of 54 after recovering from a debilitating case of Lyme disease that served as a wake-up call. She walked away from a successful real estate career that paid the bills but brought no joy, threw a backpack over her shoulder, and headed out to pursue her true passions of travel, writing, and photography. Today she travels the world full time, taking stunning photos and writing about her amazing adventures on her blog, *Hole In The Donut Cultural Travel*.

My mother went back to school at 48 to get her master's degree in nursing. At 51, she started her career as a Nurse Practitioner. "I might have twenty years of practice ahead of me," she told me. "I can do a lot of good in twenty years."

I recently attended a fundraiser at a college seminary near my home. The man who served our table was a first-year student, but he appeared to be older than my parents. He introduced himself to us and told us a little about his background: he'd spent 18 years as a teacher before deciding to become a priest.

When I was in high school, my 70-year-old grandmother sold her Chicago home and drove to Florida to start a new life for herself. Her husband had died a few years earlier and she was tired of dealing with the cold. My mom was horrified that her own mother would move so far away so late in life, but Nana was adamant that this was the best time to make the change. "I'm not going to sit here and just wait to die," she told us.

Why should any of us sit here and wait to die? As long as we are breathing, we have the opportunity to try something new and to do things differently. Whether we have 20 days or 20 years ahead of us, we have time to learn, grow, and experience the rush of novelty. It's never too late for growth or happiness.

8

There's No Such Thing As A Sure Thing

Now that I've shared with you the inspiring stories of people who tried new things and discovered their passion and life's purpose in the process, I have to remind you that change doesn't always work out that perfectly. The reason we instinctively shy away from change is because it's risky. Sometimes things do, in fact, end badly.

Sometimes you quit your job to start a business and you find out you can't get a loan, the market's saturated, and the economy is on the downhill slide. Sometimes you spend months writing a novel, submit to publishers, and receive nothing but boiler-plate rejection letters in return. Sometimes you open yourself up to a new friend before finding out they're a world-class creep. Not all risks end up in the win column; that's what makes them risks.

But, and forgive the cliché here, you never know until you try.

You never know if you're an artist if you never pick up

the brush. You never know if that new co-worker is your soul mate if you don't introduce yourself. You never know if you're a crafting genius if you don't go ahead and turn on the sewing machine.

Experimenting Leads To Clarity

One of the biggest obstacles standing between us and happiness is how much we don't know about what makes us happy. Despite all the research that's been done and the books that have been written, we're still mostly left to figure out on our own how to be happy. That's because happiness is not universal; your bliss could bore me to tears.

Where do we start? How do we begin to identify what makes us happy?

We can start by experimenting with novelty. Try new things and see what sticks. Trial and error is not a fast track to happiness, but it's helpful when it comes to discovering what makes you tick. Of course, the next question is: what do you try first?

Let's Play The Lottery Game

My husband used to go on for hours about what he would do if he won the lottery, and I would get furious. It was, I told him, a complete waste of time and served to do nothing but remind me of all the things we did not have and could not do. These daydreaming marathons of his left me frustrated and disappointed rather than inspired. "If you're not happy," I would tell him, "why don't you spend that mental energy on something that could actually happen?"

So, I would totally understand if you were inclined to skip this exercise altogether and chalk it up to stupid mind games that produce nothing in the real world. I get it.

But I've learned in the last couple of years that this can

actually be a pretty useful first step, especially if you're feeling really stuck. It requires a certain amount of bravery; you have to trust that there will be a way for you to experience parts of these things you dream up. You have to have faith that you are not given desires and passions because God likes to screw with you, but because you are *meant* to be happy.

The dream of winning the lottery (or being financially independent or debt free) is almost never about *having* piles of money. How many of us have fantasized about swimming in pools of money Scrooge McDuck style? OK, fine, maybe that would be cool. Once. Maybe twice. *But then what?*

Chances are, the real lottery fantasy is about what you would *do* with the money. Or maybe it's really about what you would do if you didn't have to worry about money and the bills that it pays.

Ask yourself:

- What would you do today if you had unlimited funds available?

- What would you do for the next six months if you didn't have to worry about paying your bills?

- What would you do if you had a universal remote and could just push pause on all of the deadlines and due dates and responsibilities in your life?

Begin your novelty experiments by doing something from your dream day. Look for pieces you can implement right now. If you dream about travel, go for a road trip this weekend or tour a local museum after work. If you dream about becoming an author, then write on your lunch break.

Paint. Create. Play with your kids. Skype with your best friend.

Take these first steps and you'll have happier days at the very least. You'll get those moments of euphoria, even if your entire life hasn't changed. Keep doing the things that sound cool, the things that you dream about, and your life may in fact be transformed over time.

I can't tell you how it will turn out for you. I can't tell you that you'll discover you have a passion for building model trains and will someday be able to quit your job and open a successful hobby shop. I can't tell you that starting an herb garden will lead to you becoming a horticulture expert on national talk shows. You may find that you hate model trains, or realize your greatest agriculture success is having fresh basil. I have no idea what your exact path is.

But you will know it. If you follow the road that is littered with the things you love, and learn all about the things that were much cooler in your dreams than in reality, you will eventually find that you're walking down the right path. And you probably won't recognize it until you're already halfway down, when you turn around and look behind you and go "Ohhh, so this is what purpose looks like." You will have that moment, eventually, if you take those first blind steps in faith.

It's Worth A Shot

Even though our experiments aren't guaranteed to work out the way we think, and they're almost certain to make us uncomfortable at some point, I still believe that embracing novelty, change, and growth can lead us to happiness. Cultivating a habit of novelty helps us get used to the discomfort of change, a skill that we need to create long-term happiness. Playing with new possibilities also increases the odds that we'll stumble across the things we most need to learn about ourselves.

Sometimes that's how happiness works. We open up to learning about how snowflakes are formed and we accidentally discover that we're afraid of being alone. We move to a new state because we think a new job will make us happy, and we end up realizing that a whole lot of our parenting decisions had been based on what our neighbors might think of us. Life lessons are usually unexpected and unpredictable.

Don't be afraid to try new things even if you don't think you've fully embraced where or who you are. Don't avoid novelty because you question your motives or worry you aren't ready. Don't avoid jumping in because you aren't sure you know the difference between an intrinsic goal or an extrinsic goal, or because you're afraid that you're chasing a feeling that won't last. It's always OK to try.

You might find that you are constantly trying new things for a while. You might feel like a flake because nothing seems to "stick." You might suspect that you're running or hiding or approaching this whole business of life wrong. But you will figure it out. As long as you show up and try, you will find your way - and you'll have a lot of great stories to tell about the journey you took to get there.

Suggested Next Steps

As you work towards happiness using the map of Growth, consider taking some of these steps in your daily life:

- Make a small change to your daily routine: take a different way to work, have lunch in a new restaurant, or just brush your teeth with your non-dominant hand.

- Look for opportunities to say yes.

- Read frequently.

- Take a free class or attend a seminar.

- Eat new foods.

- Make something with your hands.

Looking for more action steps? Every week I share a new happiness challenge online. These tiny assignments are based on science, research, and experience. Check out the latest challenge at http://inpursuitofhappiness.net/weekly-challenge/.

Map Notes

THE THIRD MAP: GRATITUDE

"Do not spoil what you have by desiring what you have not; remember that what you now have was once among the things you only hoped for."

— Epicurus

9

The Science Of Gratitude

While the previous map suggests ways to discover new types of happiness, the Gratitude map will help you recognize happiness when you see it. Gratitude also expands the happiness you already have.

Most of us would agree that gratitude is a good thing. We encourage it in our children and appreciate it from those whom we help. What you may not do is make gratitude a priority in your life, something that's as crucial to your happiness as eating is to your survival. Gratitude can sustain you, but much like a healthy diet, it's most beneficial when applied consistently and continually instead of in spurts around holidays. It takes a bit of effort and commitment, but science tells us that the rewards are definitely worth the work.

Dr. Robert Emmons wrote the book on the science of gratitude. Literally. It's called *Thanks! How the New Science of Gratitude Can Make You Happier,* and it offers empirical proof of what most of us instinctively know to be true: thankful people are happier people. Dr. Emmons's research reveals that gratitude contributes to a happier life not just by creating a short-term burst of happiness, but also because it fosters the habits and characteristics that help us to be peaceful, loving, generous, and successful people.

We usually hear the word "gratitude" or "grateful" for the first time when we're children and our parents are trying to get us to stop asking for more. It turns out that Mom and Dad were on the right track and that we would indeed have been less demanding if we had spent more time giving thanks. Gratitude has been linked to a decrease in envy and a reduced interest in material goods. Grateful people are less likely to use possessions to measure success or self-worth, and are more likely to share what they do have. It makes sense - the more energy you put into loving what you have, the less attention you have to devote to coveting what you don't.

It's important to note, however, that gratitude is not simply a way for people who have less to learn to be satisfied with their inferior lots in life. In fact, research suggests that gratitude is a common trait among successful people and one that can help you achieve your personal and professional goals. Practicing gratitude can also increase alertness, enthusiasm, determination, attentiveness, and energy, all characteristics that can contribute to achievement. So not only does gratitude help you appreciate what you have, it may make it easier for you to obtain what you want.

Finally, and perhaps most importantly, gratitude can improve your relationships, which are believed to be one of the strongest indicators of happiness. People who actively engage in gratitude tend to be compassionate, empathetic, and more connected to other people. According to Emmons, gratitude helps us appreciate unearned rewards. We aren't listing our accomplishments, but rather acknowledging what we've been freely given. Perhaps this helps us recognize our own inherent worthiness, which makes it easier to see that same quality in others. It's no wonder grateful people are also perceived as being helpful, which no doubt makes others more eager to hang out with them.

What Is Gratitude?

When I asked my seven-year-old daughter what gratitude was, she said it was "a feeling, like happiness or something." If asked the same question, you might use the words "thankful" or "appreciate" to describe gratitude. Dictionary.com defines gratitude as "the quality or feeling of being grateful or thankful." I would suggest that the gratitude that makes us happier, however, is even more than a feeling.

When researchers like Dr. Emmons attempt to study the effects of gratitude, they don't simply ask their participants if they feel thankful. Most of the experiments I've read about involve an *action* of gratitude. Research subjects might be asked to make a list of good things, or even to simply describe their current surroundings. The method varies, but the motivation is the same - in order for gratitude to have measurable results, it must be practiced. Gratitude that has been proven to have an impact, then, is something you do as much as it's something you feel.

While researchers focus on gratitude that can be measured, psychologists are careful to distinguish between gratitude and indebtedness. Indebtedness describes the feeling of needing to pay back or make up for the good that you received. Gratitude, on the other hand, does not involve balancing any cosmic scales. Instead, it is a simple act of recognizing and acknowledging goodness. Although both gratitude and indebtedness can be triggered by generosity or good fortune, gratitude makes us feel happy while indebtedness is believed to make us feel bad. People who feel indebted experience stress, guilt, and anxiety about proving their worth. Where gratitude affirms our inherent worth, indebtedness insists it must be earned and makes us fearful that we will fall short.

It's important to point out here that a belief in one's worthiness is not the same as entitlement. Entitlement suggests that you are *owed* happiness by the world, whereas worthiness says that you *deserve* to be happy. The difference is subtle but crucial. When you know you are worthy, you can appreciate happiness without feeling guilty that you've been blessed too much or given more than your fair share. You can enjoy and celebrate the good instead of fearing retribution for being disproportionately rewarded. That doesn't mean that you expect everyone to give you anything or that you give up responsibility for your happiness.

Do not think you have to cross the line into indebtedness in order to avoid entitlement. It's possible to be appreciative without feeling a desperate need to make it up to the world. And, according to the experts, you and everyone around you will be better off if you can learn to do exactly that.

A Focus On Small Things

In 2013, the Happier company released an iPhone app designed to help people practice gratitude. Users are encouraged to document three moments each day that make them feel grateful, and to share those moments with others. Founder Nataly Kogan says that the idea for the app came from poring over much of the research about happiness.

I spoke with Nataly six months after she'd launched the company. One of the things she said that she had learned about happiness through the process of developing and using the Happier app was that "the smaller moments often have more of an impact on how I feel than the big accomplishments."

Our big moments tend to be those accomplishments towards which we work. We anticipate them, plan for them, and sacrifice for them. And then, when they arrive, we hopefully take the time to celebrate them. The small things, however, tend to be recognized rather than achieved.

It's up to us to notice the generosity in a co-worker bringing us a cup of coffee. We choose to appreciate the beauty of the changing leaves on a fall day. We can make a point of cherishing the weight of a child's head on our shoulder. Practicing gratitude for the small things is a willful act, and one that teaches us that happiness can be both sought and found.

"Finding gratitude in small things showed me that it's possible to see the world through a different lens," Nataly said. Focusing your gratitude on small things also lets you enjoy happiness between the big moments. It helps you weave happiness into you everyday life and consistently enjoy the benefits of gratitude. It also puts happiness at your disposal at all times, because you can always find at least one small thing to be grateful for.

10

Create A Gratitude Practice

A gratitude practice is one of those things that sounds kind of stupid and simple, but can have a dramatic impact on your life if you just close your eyes and try it for a little bit. Really.

I learned about gratitude practices from Karen Walrond, a blogger and author who, by the time I met her, seemed to just ooze positivity. She seemed like the kind of person for whom gratitude would be easy: she works for herself as a photographer, speaker, and writer, and she has a happy and healthy family. She wrote a book, *The Beauty of Different*, about the various features that make every person uniquely beautiful. It's almost expected that she spends time everyday writing in her journal about how thankful she is for her amazing life. As it turns out, however, Karen learned about gratitude when life wasn't so rosy.

"Gratitude saved my life," Karen says.

About 15 years before Karen was a full-time writer, speaker, and photographer, she was a young law-school graduate who'd just taken her bar exams. Before the results came in the mail, she was laid-off from her first law job.

Around the same time, she and her husband decided to divorce. She felt like giving up. Lying in bed one night, she made a deal with herself that she would keep going if she could come up with one thing for which she was grateful. She remembered a delicious hard-boiled egg she'd eaten that day and resolved to give thanks for it. That hard-boiled egg started a daily habit that would continue for more than 17 years and follow Karen through a successful law career, a new marriage, and a transition to a more fulfilling life as a writer and speaker.

My Gratitude Practice

I started my gratitude practice as a marketing gimmick for my blog one month into my year-long road trip. I imagined readers would copy my "Happiness Highlights" posts and link to my blog when they did their own. At the very least, I figured I'd have a weekly feature that I could solicit sponsorship for. Unfortunately, no company ever decided to pay me to talk about what made me happy, and "Happiness Highlights" didn't become a viral sensation that brought thousands of visitors to my blog. In fact, those Monday posts didn't even get very many comments, but they changed my outlook on life.

In the beginning, I posted photos and stories from the places we visited while driving around America. Because the new experiences were the cause of most of my happiness in the early days of my trip, the series read more like a travelogue than any sort of gratitude journal. After several weeks, however, the novelty began to wear off and reality set in.

Living in a 24-foot travel trailer with a grown man and two not-so-small children is not the glamorous experience you might imagine. There's a lot of... closeness. In our case, there was also a lot of worrying about when the money would run out and getting the kids used to online schooling with their dad. It wasn't always fun, and we went through a shaky transition period. It was during those days of wondering which one of us would snap first that I began to really feel the power of the gratitude practice.

Every Sunday night, I would sit down to write my "Happiness Highlights" post. Many nights, I would be fuming when I opened the laptop, having just fought with the kids about something I wasn't willing to spend money on or argued with Jared about how he should be doing a better job of planning the kids' curriculum for the week. And then I would open Wordpress and have to come up with something for which I was grateful.

I would scroll through my Twitter and Facebook feeds from the previous week and revisit all the pictures I'd taken. As I relived my recent past, I'd skim over the rough patches and focus on the happiest and most beautiful memories. By the time I was finished with my post, I was inevitably less angry and feeling lighter for having remembered the good parts of my week. In Gretchen Rubin's book *The Happiness Project*, she writes, "To eke out the most happiness from an experience, we must anticipate it, savor it as it unfolds, express happiness, and recall a happy memory." My gratitude practice, I realized, was forcing me to regularly recall my happiest memories.

As the months wore on, my weekly gratitude practice also helped with another of Rubin's requirements for eking out the most happiness: I began to anticipate it. Because I knew I was going to be compiling a collection of happiness highlights, I kept my eye out for them. I made a point of capturing it in some way (savor it as it unfolds) - either by taking a photo, updating a social media account, or making a note for myself - so that I would remember to write about it later (express happiness).

I maintained my weekly online gratitude practice for over a year, and it shifted my perspective from that of always looking forward to one of constantly looking around for blessings to count. I learned not only to appreciate what I had, but to treasure it. And, I learned how to skim over the rough patches when I needed to find something good.

Create Your Own Gratitude Practice

While I wholeheartedly believe, in part because of my own experience, that consistently listing the things for which you are grateful can make you happier, I also know that taking on any new habit – even one as simple as saying thank you – can seem overwhelming at first. I suggest making it easier on yourself by following a few basic steps to create a personalized practice that you'll actually be able to keep up with.

1. **Choose your medium.** There are numerous ways to make an accounting of your blessings. You could:

    - Post a photo to Instagram
    - Write a blog post
    - Keep a journal
    - Add a notation to your daily planner
    - Make a video

    Choose a method that you'll enjoy and realistically have time for on a consistent basis. Consider how you feel most comfortable expressing yourself. If you enjoy writing, a blog post or nightly notes in a journal might be a natural solution. If you're a more visual person, taking photos with your phone might be a good fit.

2. **Designate a time for gratitude.** This is another one of those steps that sounds lame, but if you skip it, there's a good chance you'll end up dropping the whole exercise within a few days. Take the time to decide when, exactly, you'll practice gratitude.

3. **Tie the practice to something you already do.** For example, if you read in bed every night, try making a note in your gratitude journal before you pick up the book. You could update a blog before checking email in the morning, or post a photo at the beginning of your lunch break.

4. **Do it when you don't feel grateful.** Make a commitment to yourself to practice gratitude every day for a month, even when you're having a bad day. These are the times when searching for at least one thing for which to be grateful will have the biggest effect.

You might not notice any "results" at first, but change happens over time. Resolve to be consistently grateful for one month and you just might find yourself feeling happier.

11

Minimalism As A Gratitude Practice

I accidentally stumbled upon the idea of minimalism as an act of gratitude when we decided to move from a 3,000-square-foot house into a 192-square-foot travel trailer. Although minimalism wasn't a preset goal of our road trip, it was an inevitable byproduct of four people living in a small space. While I was engaged in a weekly gratitude practice on my blog, my entire family was participating in this daily experiment of living with less stuff. The unexpected result of embracing the concept was an increased awareness of and appreciation for what we had.

It was pretty cool to realize, for example, that we could spend an entire evening laughing and connecting to one another using no more than a single deck of cards. We also learned to cook without an oven, which forced us to seek out new recipes. My husband in particular loved learning how spices could add variety to a few simple ingredients, and he developed a passion for Indian food. Having fewer clothes encouraged everyone, including our kids, to take better care of their favorite pieces. The longer we lived with less, the more I noticed everyone moving away from a disposable mentality.

A little more than a year after moving out of our house in the suburbs of Central Florida, we moved out of the RV and into a rental in the city of Pittsburgh. Our goal when we moved in was to maintain a pretty minimalist lifestyle and, hopefully, hold on to our appreciation for the simple pleasures. That hasn't been as easy as I expected.

One of Jared's favorite things to do is dig through other people's junk. According to Foursquare, he's the mayor of every thrift store in a 20-mile radius of our home, and he can tell you which estate sale company has the best pricing. I think he has Craigslist bookmarked on his iPad. I admit that it is fun to see what trash you can turn into treasure, and I have spent many Saturday mornings bargain hunting with him. But, I have also tried to be careful during our expeditions to only pick up things I'd already decided I wanted before I left the house and to stick with my monthly budget (something that is easy to do because we only use cash). But, Jared gets frustrated by these restrictions sometimes.

"It's such a good deal!" he'll say.

"But we don't need two more couches," I remind him.

"Man, I can't believe I'm out of money. Those jeans are awesome!"

"But you were completely happy before you saw those jeans," I say, "and remember all the great stuff you bought with that money you no longer have?"

Not buying more isn't just about saving money or working towards sainthood, it's about remembering to appreciate what I already have. It's about not letting outside forces create a hole in my life where there wasn't one before.

As I told Jared one day when I was explaining why I wouldn't be upgrading my iPhone to the latest model, "I love my phone. I loved it two days ago before the iPhone 5 came out, and I still love it."

I already have so much, and I have the means to acquire more. I have what I need and what I want, and I can easily provide my children with both. I have the luxury of choosing between going with or without. What a gift! What a rare, precious gift in a world where so many people make do – and sometimes don't – with so much less. What a tragedy it would be to forget to be grateful in the face of all I already have. Sometimes, I think, the best way to remember how lucky we are is to resist the urge to have more.

Resisting The Call For More

In 2003, Rachel Jonat was an elite athlete working towards a spot on the Olympic rowing team. She describes her life then as glamorous from the outside, with frequent travel to Europe and occasional appearances in the media, but says that she was constantly focused on what was missing. "I wasn't the top athlete and I struggled financially." Having grown up in a family that never seemed to have enough money, the anxiety was familiar to Rachel. "I grew up feeling I never got enough or had enough." In 2010, Rachel made a decision that helped her finally break the never-enough cycle.

After spending 10 months at home on maternity leave, Rachel found herself overwhelmed by all of the stuff that filled her family's 1100-square-foot condo. "Our junk was everywhere," she told me. Encouraged by minimalist blogs and a goal to pay off $80,000 in consumer debt, Rachel and her husband jumped head first into the process of simplifying their lives. "For four months I purged and purged. I took carload after carload of housewares, clothing and electronics to the Salvation Army to donate. I sold my wedding dress. I sold the torch I ran with in the 2010 Winter Olympic Torch Relay on eBay. We eventually sold our car."

The result, Rachel said, was a newfound sense of calm in her own home. The space was easier to clean, and her family was able to save a ton of money by reducing their spending on household items and clothes. More importantly, Rachel, who now maintains a successful website at TheMinimalistMom. com, finally felt like she had enough. "Getting rid of 50% of our possessions actually made me feel like I had more," she said. "I couldn't see how much I did have when I was so focused on what everyone else had that I did not."

That's one of the reasons minimalism is such a powerful catalyst for gratitude; it helps us break the habit of comparing our stuff with everyone else's. When you're purposefully trying to minimize how much you have, you stop looking at what everyone else has as a benchmark for how successful you are. When you're no longer casting about to see what you're supposed to buy next, you're free to appreciate all that you already have. In Rachel's case, that includes a life focused on people rather than items that need dusting. "I have my health, my family and we have the means to live a pretty great lifestyle: we live by the sea, I'm able to work part-time and I have a lot of free time to spend with my husband and children."

Minimalism And Mindfulness

Living with less can be a powerful reminder to appreciate what we have. But for many of us, getting rid of the things we own will only take us so far because we can quickly replace it all on our next trip to Target. The process of buying new things, as I learned when we moved out of the RV, has become an almost habitual act for much of the Western world. And it's not just how we spend our money, but where we spend much of our time.

Elizabeth Liu began going to the mall as a way to fill time after she moved to a new city with her husband. In the absence of friendships to nurture, it became compulsive to stop by a store and pick up a few things. As she approached her 30th birthday, Elizabeth noticed she was spending almost all of her free time shopping, and she needed a change. "Shopping was very deeply ingrained in my day-to-day routine," Liu told me. She decided to take radical action: she wouldn't buy anything for one year, and she would blog about her experience to hold herself accountable.

I spoke with Elizabeth about 18 months after her experiment and asked her what she'd learned from the experience. "You can do with a lot less than what you think you can," she said. "And I was OK with not having more." When she returned to shopping after the 12-month hiatus, she had a new approach. "Now I only buy things I absolutely love," she said. "I was a big impulse shopper before, and now I sit on it and think about it." But that, Elizabeth said, wasn't the most important thing she gained from her shopping ban.

"Not shopping for a year made me mindful of what I can do with my time," Elizabeth told me. "I connected with what I actually want to do. By not spending money, I got the gift of time."

Elizabeth's revelation about time surprised me. My own efforts to buy less had made me more conscious of the stuff that cluttered my physical space, but Elizabeth's experiment had sharpened her awareness and appreciation for how she was spending her life. Listening to her story, I realized that many of us are just as careless with our hours as we are with our dollars.

We are creatures of habit, and it's easy for us to slip into routines that have little to do with our values and more to do with maintaining a status quo. We spend many of our days buying without thinking, and our homes are filled with more than we know. Even people who don't consider themselves shopaholics tend to spend large chunks of their weekends in the local big box store. Maybe the real power of minimalism, as with gratitude, is the heightened sense of awareness that it gives us.

Courtney Carver writes the popular minimalism blog *Be More With Less* and agrees that minimalism can lead to happiness as a byproduct of awareness and gratitude. Carver, who adopted minimalism in response to an MS diagnosis in 2006, told me, "I've always been a semi-grateful person, even before I recognized that I had too much. But since eliminating a lot of what isn't important to me, I find I have more time and awareness to be grateful."

Courtney recommends making space for gratitude in our lives, both physically and on the calendar, if we want to be happier. "Making space for the gratitude is the first step," she says. "You can set aside five minutes in the morning or by pulling over to a park on your lunch break instead of answering 40 voice mails. Then maybe you can clear a spot in a room so that you have a place to practice gratitude."

Making a list of good things in a journal every day may cause you to notice what is good. Deciding not to go to a mall for one year might force someone to consciously decide where she will go instead. Choosing to go without helps me see what I have. But the method is secondary to the results. It is the noticing, deciding, and seeing that brings happiness closer.

12

Depression Is Not A Lack Of Gratitude

In December of 2008, we took our son, Devin, to Disney World to celebrate his eighth birthday. After two hours, I found myself standing in front of Cinderella's castle, with ice cream on my shirt, sobbing. We went home early, and I wondered if *maybe* I was suffering from some sort of depression.

I have a family history of depression, but that didn't make it any easier to admit that there was something wrong with the way my brain works. I didn't want to live with that diagnosis or the stigma that still accompanies mental health issues. So, I tried to make myself be not depressed.

I read self-help books. I watched Oprah. I tried to will myself to be grateful for all that I had. I held my children, told my husband I loved him, and laid awake at night trying to make a mental list of everything that should be making me happy. I still came painfully close to driving my car into a guard rail on my way home from work one afternoon.

Between the Disney World meltdown and the guard rail

fantasy, it was clear I needed help. Medical help. Drugs. I made an appointment with a primary care provider whose name I found on my insurance company's website - a doctor chosen only because of her proximity to my office - and begged my husband to go with me.

That initial appointment was a disaster. I spent 15 minutes tearfully relaying my symptoms, the suicidal thoughts and the crushing feelings of hopelessness, while the doctor looked at her clipboard and her watch. "So, you want anti-depressants then?" she asked when I had finished.

"I... uh... I think, if you think that sounds like depression," I stammered, ashamed to be caught clamoring for drugs in front of Jared.

"Sure, probably. What kind do you want?"

I gave her the name of an anti-depressant I'd recently seen advertised on TV, and she wrote me a prescription. I was humiliated and angry, but I was also desperate. I filled the script and began taking the new medication immediately. Within a week or so, I noticed a difference: I no longer felt like I needed to die.

I tell you this because it is important to know that there are some things you can't practice your way out of. Depression, which is mistakenly used as the antonym of happiness, cannot be cured with a gratitude journal. But it makes you think you should be able to do just that.

For years, I wondered what the hell was wrong with me that I didn't appreciate my life. How could a woman with two healthy children and a loving husband want to kill herself? How could I have such horribly selfish thoughts? Experts would tell me to focus outward and count my blessings, but I could not muster anything that resembled hope.

That's how depression works. It disconnects your feelings

from reality and erases your ability to hope.

Getting on anti-depressants did not make me happy. Even seeing a good doctor who took the time to get me on the right anti-depressants didn't make me happy. It made me not suicidal. It made me able to get out of bed and get dressed every day. In time, the medication made me able to feel the effects of gratitude and allowed my brain to think that maybe I could figure out how to be happier.

It's estimated that depression affects about 15 million Americans each year. Some common symptoms of depression include changes in appetite, changes in sleep patterns, fatigue, lack of motivation, and trouble concentrating. The symptoms can be a bit ambiguous, and there's no blood test or x-ray picture that can diagnose it. That's one of the reasons it's so tempting to turn to "self help" as a means of treating it.

If you suspect you may be suffering from depression, if gratitude and self discovery aren't working, and no self-help book in the world is making you feel less hopeless, the best next step is to seek professional help. Thoughts of suicide are always a sign that you need more than a book or pep talk to turn things around.

This is one of the only times when I will recommend a universal solution. No one can will themselves out of depression. Contact a doctor, a psychiatrist if possible. If you've thought about committing suicide, call the National Suicide Prevention Lifeline at 1-800-273-8255.

And mostly, know that your despair is not a result of you being ungrateful.

Suggested Next Steps

As you work towards happiness using the map of Gratitude, consider taking some of these steps in your daily life:

- Create a gratitude practice.
- Send thank you notes.
- Go on a shopping hiatus.
- Download the Happier app.

Looking for more action steps? Every week I share a new happiness challenge online. These tiny assignments are based on science, research, and experience. Check out the latest challenge at http://inpursuitofhappiness.net/weekly-challenge/.

Map Notes

THE FOURTH MAP: SELF DISCOVERY

"At the center of your being you have the answer; you know who you are and you know what you want."

— Lao Tzu

.

12

The Importance Of Navel Gazing

I am a born navel gazer. Since I was a child, I have spent hours every day lost inside my head, wondering about who I am. I analyze my feelings, my thoughts, my habits - all of it. There are few subjects as interesting to me as me.

I realize this internal focus is not something everyone shares, nor something everyone desires. In fact, looking inward often gets a bad rap. Words like "selfish" and "narcissism" may make you leery of spending too much attention on your own inner workings. But you don't need to fear self awareness. In fact, an honest picture of who you are can be good for your mental health and well-being. Of course, that's not how it started for me.

My obsession with self awareness was borne mostly of fear. I have always been afraid that I would be surprised by an attack on my faults if I remained oblivious to them. I dread the humiliation that comes from discovering something unlikeable about yourself by way of someone else not liking you. I guess I assumed that knowing my faults would allow me to either brace myself for rejection or fix myself in order to prevent that pain entirely.

Self discovery as a means of perfecting myself in order to gain outside approval did not serve me well. Shocking, I know. Instead of trying to know myself, I used my reflections to constantly judge and criticize. I wasn't on a journey of self discovery; I was on a witch hunt. I was pretty sure there was something wrong with me and that if I studied myself with enough painful honesty, I'd be able to figure it out and fix it. When you go searching for a problem, you're guaranteed to find one. I found plenty.

My Love Affair With Approval

My quest for things to fix inside myself came to a temporary end after my second child was born, but not because I'd had any epiphany about self acceptance. On the day my daughter was born, I was asked to be in a wedding that would take place in three months. Determined not to be the fat bridesmaid, I started a strict low-carb diet and lost the baby fat I'd accumulated through two pregnancies and the freshman 15 I'd picked up at college five years earlier. I was the thinnest I'd been since hitting puberty, and people noticed.

A funny thing happens when you lose weight: people suddenly feel comfortable telling you how fat you were before. Everywhere I went in our small town, people congratulated me on my newly acceptable appearance. I was a little surprised at how happy everyone seemed for me, but I was thrilled to have so much approval coming at me.

Around the same time, I started working at a radio station about 30 minutes away. This was the first time in my adult life I'd worked with people who hadn't known me since high school, and it would become my first exposure to male attention. *I got hit on.* People talked to me as if I knew I was attractive. This was a completely new experience for me, and I started to wonder what the hell was wrong with everyone else (i.e. my husband) that they didn't see how amazing I was.

And then, I started blogging.

Practically overnight, I became the popular girl I'd never been able to be in high school. People told me every single day that I was pretty, funny, and talented. I stretched my creative muscles and shook my virtual ass as much as I could, and the compliments kept coming. I had never felt so loved, so worthy, so appreciated and approved of.

The Problem With External Approval

That heady feeling of being the Queen Bee of the Universe lasted a few months before the foundation began to crack. Rumors started to swirl at work, and men who flirted with me in meetings plotted to steal my clients. On the Internet, voices of dissent began to rise up among all the praise. People said I was immature, a bad wife, and probably a horrible mother. I fought to defend myself, desperate to hang on to the virtual stamp of approval.

But here's the thing I learned about external approval: it's fickle. A new girl in the office can steal your attention and admiration, and an online fan can decide to launch a hate site about you because you didn't respond to her emails. And there's nothing you can do about it. It's not that other people are bad, it's that their opinions can't be controlled and really have very little to do with who you are. I learned that the hard way.

After I exploded my marriage, there was no shortage of critics and vultures eager to pick at any gory details they could find (or make up). The same people who had cheered for me when I danced on the virtual stage roared with glee when I fell on my ass. And no amount of explaining or healing or personal growth would change the stories they told themselves about me.

In the smoking ashes of my life, I learned about a different kind of self examination. After disappointing everyone who mattered to me, it seemed pointless to continue the never-ending quest for approval. I'd failed. The only thing left to do was start over and try and figure out who the hell I was apart from the audience reactions. That's when I began to understand the difference between looking for fault and searching for understanding.

Turning Inward

In the last few years, I have benefited greatly from my journeys of self discovery. The more I have learned about myself, the easier it has become for me to like - and even love - myself. In fact, understanding myself better has helped me care less about how other people perceive me. I know who I am, and the opinions of an outside observer carry less weight than my own.

One of the best reasons to engage in self discovery is to debunk the myth that there is something wrong with you. None of us are perfect, but some of us carry around a laundry list of things that we think are broken or inherently bad inside us. Most of the time, this laundry list is based more in fear than in reality. Learning about ourselves helps us see the difference between who our insecurities tell us we are and who we really are.

Awareness also helps us see what we react to. So many of the things we feel, think, say, and do stem from a reaction to a fear or belief, and it'd be nice to at least know what it is we're responding to. We may even be able to change how we feel, think, speak, and act if we can more clearly see the catalysts.

The benefits of self discovery extend beyond the esoteric and airy fairy. Logically, knowing yourself is an important aspect of success and happiness. If you want to be happier than you are right now, then you might need to make some changes. You can't change what you don't understand. Even if you don't want to change, the constant motion of life demands adaptation. The better you know yourself, the more easily you will be able to adjust yourself so that you can continue to be happy in a dynamic world.

Self discovery allows me to soar with my strengths and compensate for my weaknesses. It also helps me to more clearly define my personal version of happiness and to know how I might best achieve it.

Are You Self Aware?

A therapist once told me that if I took the time to ask if I was self aware, I probably had nothing to worry about. People who don't look inward don't wonder about their state of awareness (and they probably don't buy books about happiness). That doesn't mean, however, that you don't have a lot to learn about yourself. None of us know ourselves entirely. Because we are always changing, there is always more to uncover. Self discovery is an ongoing journey that constantly yields new benefits.

The goal is not to discover yourself - check! - and then achieve happiness – check, check! It is the *process* of self discovery that brings you to happiness. And in discovering who you are, you will learn that you are worth getting to know better.

13

Challenge Your Values

I always assumed I knew what my values were, but I realized when I was going through my separation that I'd spent most of my life trying to make decisions based on what I thought I was supposed to value. Those values weren't necessarily good or bad, I just hadn't taken the time to decide if they were *mine*.

As I struggled to decide if I wanted a divorce, I had to ask myself if I actually valued matrimony, monogamy, and life-long partnership. Did I really think those things were crucial, or had I just automatically bought into what I'd been told?

My therapist walked me through the history of marriage. She used historical facts to challenge my preconceived ideas of marriage being biblically based. Her goal wasn't to prove me wrong, but to push me to question myself. I read about the development of marriage as a contract between landowners and looked for stories from people who spent their lives in committed, not-married relationships. I pursued all the angles, looked at all the available facts, and let the mess of it all sit in my gut for a while.

I decided that marriage was a beautiful choice, but not one that was crucial to the survival of my soul. After weeks of reconsideration, I chose to embrace both my marriage and my vows, but I did so with much more awareness than I had on my wedding day. While some might say my search was blasphemous, I'm more confident in my ability to actually live the version of marriage that I've taken on. I've made it mine by daring to take a closer look, by taking a chance that I would discover something that made me feel wrong.

In the last few years, I've gone through a similar process with a lot of my values. I've questioned my feelings on education, community, success, financial stability, leadership, justice, home, and friendship. Sometimes I've ended up back in the same place I started - like when we chose to go back to non-mobile living after trying out the nomad route for a while - and other times I've decided to let go of things I used to deem necessary. For example, I'm no longer concerned with making sure my kids attend college. I think it would be great if they do, but I no longer see it as crucial to their future success or happiness.

Questioning our values makes us vulnerable. We might unearth something that makes us feel stupid. We might have to loosen our grip on certainty. We may wind up so confused that we have to throw up our hands and admit we have no clue what to believe. But we may also come to an understanding that feels so right, it settles onto us like a second skin, providing strength and comfort that second-hand values never could.

To know who you are, you must know what you value. To know what you value, you must take the time to consider the alternatives. Know that it's OK to let go of a "good" value if it doesn't really and truly fit you. Removing it from your list of core beliefs doesn't mean you condemn those who hold on to it; it just means that you're figuring out your own truth.

Identifying your values means more than picking and choosing from a list of words. It also means defining what those words mean to you. For example, my daughter is friends with anyone who asks her to play, while my definition of friendship requires me to be a bit more discerning. Today, when I say that I value marriage, I mean something entirely different than I did when I said the same sentence ten years ago.

I recommend that you take the time to clearly identify your belief system for yourself. Even just making a mental note of the beliefs by which you guide your life can heighten your sense of awareness, and writing them down can give you a powerful tool for making future decisions. You don't have to get fancy or stretch your vocabulary. Just make a list of what matters to you. As you do, ask yourself if you've made those values your own by challenging them.

Writing A Mission Statement

A mission statement is basically a way to write out your values. It's also one of those tasks that I put off for years because it seemed a) kind of stupid and b) pretty difficult. Every time I would read a mission statement, whether for an organization or an individual, I was intimidated. How could everything I want, need, and care about be filtered down into one succinct paragraph or sentence?

I was prompted to bite the bullet and finally make the effort after reading an article on one of my favorite blogs, *The Liberated Life Project*. Writer Maia Duerr walked readers through the process of choosing words that resonate and then molding those into a mission statement.

Before I show you how to write a mission statement, I want to tell you why you shouldn't skip this part (because two years ago, I would have totally skipped this part). Since writing my mission statement and giving myself a concrete list of my values, I've had to make some pretty big life decisions. This declaration of what I hold dear served as a compass to show me the way.

For example, in the summer of 2012, I had to decide where my family would live after we'd sold all of our stuff and spent a year wandering. Should we play it safe and move back to our hometown in Iowa, next to family and cheap housing? Should we throw all caution to the wind and try to live in New York City? Should we move back to Florida, a place that was familiar where we could enjoy established friendships and beautiful weather? Or should we move to Pittsburgh, a city we'd unexpectedly fallen in love with that was much more affordable than the Big Apple?

When the options threatened to drown me, I turned to my mission statement:

> "My mission is to know and love myself, my neighbor, and my world and to encourage and inspire others to know and love themselves.
>
> I am at my best when I am **healthy**, **exploring**, **learning**, **inspiring**, and **connecting**. I am proactive about incorporating each of these elements into my life, for I am responsible for being happy, confident, and successful.
>
> I find opportunities to use my natural talents of communicating, both listening and sharing.
>
> I travel the world and inspire people to identify and embrace what matters most in their lives, and encourage them to reach further.

I am guided and identified by the principles of
courage, **integrity**, **kindness**, and **acceptance**.

I give my husband and children the courage
and faith to live their dreams as well as my
unconditional love.

I have faith in destiny and bravely take the path
that unfolds before me."

What stood out for me was the intention to be brave. I knew that we couldn't go back to Florida or our hometown in Iowa, because those were our easy options. I needed to be courageous and do the scary thing.

Ultimately, we decided to move to Pittsburgh because it was where our hearts called us. It gave us the opportunity to live in a city without having to work ridiculous hours trying to pay for it, two things that were important to both me and Jared.

Time and time again, I've used my mission statement to remind myself to be brave. Because of this written declaration of my values, I've chosen to pursue writing over going back to a career in marketing. It's also pushed me to go back to the gym, smile at strangers, and say yes to unexpected opportunities. Decisions big and small have been made easier because I have a black and white guide to direct me.

OK, now that I've shown you my squishy insides, are you ready to put yours in writing?

How To Write A Mission Statement

1. Look at this list of words and write down on a separate piece of paper any that resonate with you.

Building	Creating
Encouraging	Communicating
Connecting	Embracing
Exploring	Giving
Healing	Helping
Integrating	Leading
Learning	Loving
Organizing	Relating
Restoring	Teaching

2. Look at the list you've created, and write a number between 1 and 5 next to each word that indicates how strongly you feel about it. If you feel nothing, write 1. If your stomach does somersaults, write 5. The words that have a 4 or 5 next to them will form the base of your mission statement.

3. Next, finish these sentences:

    I feel great when I am _____.

    I know that I am good at _____.

    My favorite way to spend time off is

    _____.

    When I die, I want to be remembered for

    _____.

Three people I admire and aspire to be more like are _____, _____, and, _____.

The attributes I admire in them are _____, _____, and _____.

4. The final step is all you. What patterns do you see? What values, goals or talents jump out at you? Spend some time reading over your piece of paper and some more time just thinking about it. Write a few sentences down, then go live your life for a little bit. Come back to your paper and revise it, removing anything that doesn't feel quite like you.

Understand that writing a mission statement is a private, personal process. You can't get it wrong, and you don't have to show anyone else. Feel free to stop when you feel like you've got something close enough, and to make changes as you and your life evolve.

Congratulations. This is the first draft of your very own map.

14

Honor Your Preferences

In the 1999 film *Runaway Bride*, Richard Gere's character, Ike, insists that Julia Roberts' character, Maggie, a woman who keeps getting engaged but running away when it's time to say "I do," doesn't know who she is or what she wants because she doesn't know how she likes her eggs. Running through her romantic and gastronomic history, he says, "With the priest you wanted scrambled, with the deadhead it was fried, with the other guy, the bug guy, it was poached, now it's egg whites only!"

"That is called changing your mind," the cold-footed woman replies.

"No, that's called not having a mind of your own."

By the end of the movie, of course, Maggie discovers who she is - and that she likes Eggs Benedict.

When I was searching for this clip online, I found that a lot of experts had been using it as an example of what not to do in a relationship. The wisdom in the movie, they said, is in recognizing that you need to know who you are separate from your partner. While that's true, what I love most about the egg story is that it highlights the importance of preferences.

It's easy to sell the importance of values. The word is tossed around constantly by everyone from pastors to politicians. Our values define us, guide us, and carry us through life's trials. Our preferences, on the other hand, are rarely mentioned and easily dismissed. That, I think, is a mistake.

Preferences are not as serious, perhaps, as values, but they are no less important on the road to self discovery. It's your preferences - whether you're a morning person or night owl, choose chocolate or vanilla, see details or big picture ideas - that make you truly unique. Your values give you shape, but your preferences color you in, adding texture and depth to the human experience. To be able to distinguish yourself from your neighbor is to see the nuances created by your many preferences.

It's important to recognize your preferences because we use them just as frequently as our values to judge ourselves. If you choose to sleep in, you might call yourself lazy. If you prefer knitting to clubbing, you might label yourself boring. And all too often, many of us try to change or ignore our preferences in an effort to be who we think we should be.

Value work can be exhausting, but acknowledging and settling into your preferences usually results in a tremendous sense of relief. Accepting your idiosyncrasies feels like a sweet surrender after a long battle against your very nature. It's the moment you finally say "OK, fine, I'm never going to be a person who loves to run. Moving on." And then you can just be.

Author Gretchen Rubin talks frequently in her books and articles about her personal commandment to "Be Gretchen." She writes, "I have a lot of notions about what I wish I liked to do, of the subjects and occupations that I wish interested me.

But it doesn't matter what I wish I were like. I am Gretchen." She admits that this makes her both happy and sad, because we each have ideals about what we think we should be. "Being Gretchen, and accepting my true likes and dislikes, also means that I have to face the fact that I will never visit a jazz club at midnight, or hang out in artists' studios, or jet off to Paris for the weekend, or pack up to go fly-fishing on a spring dawn. I won't be admired for my chic wardrobe or be appointed to a high government office. I love fortune cookies and refuse to try foie gras."

This resonates with me because I have spent much of my adult life feeling guilty about the things that I wanted and even guiltier about the things for which I had no great passion. I like spending time alone, for example, although I suspect that a good mother cherishes family time above all else. I enjoy working, another desire I don't equate with proper parenting. Despite these natural tendencies, I once spent about 18 months trying to be a stay-at-home mom; I was secretly thrilled when our finances demanded I go back to work. The reality is that while I had no trouble mastering the schedule of a housewife, I can easily tolerate messiness and I found very little joy in afternoon errands and play dates. Being a full-time, stay-at-home parent works against my very nature, and I was never going to be truly happy in that role. Ironically, I think I've become a better parent the more I've learned to embrace my preferences, in part because I am free to lean into the things I rock at (like taking my kids on adventures).

First recognizing, and then owning, your individual preferences allows you to be the person you were uniquely created to be. Your preferences are guideposts for your destiny and your purpose. Ignoring these signs will set you up for failure and a sense that you are lacking; it's the only possible result of trying to fill a role for which you were not made.

Your preferences highlight both your weaknesses and your strengths. In a way, they show you your limitations. That's a good thing. Pretending a wall isn't there doesn't make you more likely to run through it, it just increases your chances of getting a concussion when you attempt to do the impossible. Seeing the wall for what it is, however, allows you to consider alternatives. You can scale it, go around it, or decide to build your empire on this side of it. But you can only make plans once you admit that the wall exists.

Studying your preferences is like studying a landscape you plan to navigate. The hills and valleys aren't good or bad, they just are, and they need to be considered before you plan your route. Attaching judgment to your likes and dislikes serves no purpose but to waste energy and slow you down. Understanding them, however, helps you know the best ways to pursue happiness. When you've identified your preferences, you can do more of what you like, less of what you don't like, and get help for the necessary things that are difficult for you.

Raising a daughter has helped me to honor my own preferences. As a woman, I'm keenly aware of all the ways that the world will tell Emma who she should be, and I've been trying to counteract those messages since her birth. I am constantly telling her that she can like what she wants and that she was made exactly the way she was supposed to be. I've told her it's perfectly fine that she prefers camo to pink (even though I secretly wished she'd let me dress her in princess garb) and have happily catered to her love of cars over Barbies. I've made an effort not just to tolerate her individual preferences, but to celebrate them as wonderful parts of a beautiful whole.

I've made the same effort with my son, although I've found

it's gotten more difficult as he's gotten older. When he was little, it was easy to buy him puzzles instead of basketballs and take him to the museum for his birthday instead of throwing big friend parties at the local pizza house. As he approached puberty, however, it was a little harder to accept that he prefers problems to sports and solitude to group activities. Those preferences run contrary to my own, and it can be a struggle as a parent to remember that his route to happiness may (no, *will*) differ from my own. Fortunately, he is now a teenager and has no problem calling me out if I ever slip up and try to encourage him to try something that's more *me* than *him*.

Believing that our children are purposefully and rightly made is part of the parental instinct. If you're a parent, you can use that inherent wisdom as a launchpad for honoring your own individuality. Who you are is just as worthy of protecting and celebrating as who your children are. If you don't have kids, imagine a loved one is in a relationship with a controlling jerk who constantly tells your favorite person that she needs to change. Your gut would insist that the jerk was wrong and that your friend should rise up and respect herself. Sadly, we all too often play the controlling jerk in our relationship with ourselves. We deserve better.

Your preferences matter. That doesn't mean that you should never challenge your comfort zone, try new things, or be willing to compromise. You may, as Runaway Bride Maggie asserts, even change your mind from time to time. But the journey to challenging your preferences and making a willful compromise for the good of others cannot begin until you are aware of what you prefer in the first place.

Figure out how you like your eggs.

15

The Courage To Know Yourself

Self discovery is not always a fun road trip. None of us is perfect, and uncovering our weaknesses, mistakes, shame, regret, fears, and insecurities can be an incredibly painful process. But it's worth it.

To Be Seen

One of the most romantic lines from any movie, I think, comes from the 2009 film *Avatar*. As a sign of love and affection, Jake and Neytiri say to one another, "I see you." Those three words give me goosebumps and perfectly describe what I believe most of us are searching for in our relationships.

We don't just want to be liked or loved. We crave being seen, completely, and still loved in spite of our imperfections. To have someone like the persona we present to the world is nice. It can ease our loneliness and help us feel like we belong. But, we also live in fear that the real us will be discovered and cast out. When someone really sees us, however, and accepts us completely, we don't have to be afraid. To be loved warts and all is one of the most basic human needs.

This is why I love the Catholic Church's rite of confession. It sounds horrible: go into a room with a priest and tell him every shameful thought and deed you've committed (and make no mistake, that part is extremely uncomfortable). However, what comes next makes the discomfort worth it. This man who has heard all of your sins tells you that you are forgiven and still loved. It is powerful and healing, and I've heard many Catholics aptly compare it to a bath for the soul.

It is this same cleansing acceptance that we seek when we summon the courage to see our own faults. The difference is that we're not getting love from a clergymen or a friend, but from ourselves.

Revealing Your Fears

In order to see yourself, you have to figure out how to get past your own defenses. You don't just build walls between yourself and others, but you build inner walls that help protect you from your scariest truths. We all lie to ourselves, justify our actions, and create elaborate webs that shield us from accountability and the pain of our insecurities.

In marriage counseling, my therapist used the prompt "the story I make up about myself is..." to help Jared and I identify why we had specific reactions to each other's actions. For example, when he is late and doesn't call, I get very upset. I tell him he's irresponsible, selfish or rude. I assume this is how any rational person would respond, but in examining my own insecurities I could see that I was reacting because of the story I was telling myself.

When Jared is late and doesn't call, the story I tell myself is that he doesn't think about me when he's gone. Out of sight, out of mind. He doesn't care if he hurts me. He doesn't actually love me, he's just staying married to me because that's the decent thing to do.

With that story running through my head, it's no wonder I lose my shit when he finally comes home.

In addition to showing me why I reacted to Jared's tardiness, uncovering this story also helped me see one of the fears that was hiding behind my walls: I was afraid I had tricked him into marrying me by getting pregnant, and that he didn't really love me. That's a humiliating idea to walk around with, and I'd been carrying it for almost ten years before I was able to admit it to myself. Once I was able to face it and let the wave of embarrassment and fear of unworthiness wash over me, I could start the process of letting that belief go.

I've continued to use "the story I make up about myself" as an internal prompt when I find myself reacting strongly to something. If I'm furious with a friend, getting stuck in a jealousy spiral, or having the same fight with my kids, I try to stop and ask myself what the inner story is.

I'm afraid I'm a bad friend.

I'm afraid I'm not succeeding because I don't work hard enough and I'm not smart enough.

I'm afraid my kids will blame me if they don't reach their potential.

It's no coincidence that the word "afraid" shows up in a lot of my stories. Fear, I think, is the number one reason we run away from happiness. It is perhaps the most powerful human motivator.

Facing Fear

My teenage son loves to play the computer game Minecraft. The purpose is to build things and avoid being blown up by creepers and other various mobs, bad guys who spawn in the dark, cozy up beside buildings and characters, and then blow up without warning. That's pretty much exactly how fear works.

Fear grows in the dark. Our stories become stronger and more deeply rooted in our subconscious when we cover them up. Because we work so hard to keep them unseen, we're usually taken completely by surprise when they blow up and cause destruction in our lives.

When you try to control what you're thinking, you usually end up obsessing about the thing you're trying to avoid. You might have partial success in avoiding a specific thought, but the energy needed to "think about thinking" can leave you depressed, anxious, and exhausted.

Dr. Daniel Wegner runs a research lab at Harvard that once tested whether or not people could force themselves not to think of a white bear. As you can imagine, when told not to think of a white bear, it was suddenly all the research subjects could think about. The same thing happens when you try not to think about the things that scare you. If you fear being poor, you'll become obsessed with counting pennies. If you fear being left, then you'll see signs of betrayal or abandonment everywhere. The problem is not the fear, but your extreme effort to out-muscle it. You pretend it isn't there, tell yourself it's stupid, force a smile on your face, and all you are really doing is dedicating more of your mental energy to that which you most desperately want to forget. But you can't forget what you're trying to control, because you can't control and let go at the same time.

Conversely, when you shine a light on you fears, when you find the courage to face them, they lose a significant amount of their power. When you say the story out loud, you see it for the piece of fiction that it is. Unfortunately, you can only discover this is true by seeking out the thing that you're sure will destroy you.

Your instinct is to fight or run from what can harm you, including fear. So, you have to resist your very nature in order to prove your horror stories untrue. I can't lie; this is not an easy thing to do.

Working with a therapist - one who will spot and call you on your crap - can be very helpful. I've also found writing to be useful in my efforts to expose fear. Whether I'm writing in a blog or a private journal, there is tremendous power in documenting the stories I make up about myself. Another way to shine light in the dark is to allow yourself to be vulnerable and share your fears with someone who has earned your trust.

Feel The Fear

The goal in facing the fear is not really to conquer it, but rather to feel it. Fear is just a powerful feeling, and the only thing to be done with feelings is to feel them. In discovering your hidden stories, your deepest fears, you give yourself the chance to finally feel them. Only then can you let go of the fear and begin to see and accept all the nuances of who you are.

I know it's not easy. In fact, I think willfully getting face to face with our deepest fears is one of the hardest things we can put ourselves through. Just thinking about what scares us most can cause powerful physical reactions; sweaty palms, nausea, and dry mouth can all be attempts to usher us back into the land of safe and secure.

This is why it takes courage to be happy. You have to be willing to push past the obstacles that keep you stagnating. You have to choose to be afraid and act anyway. You don't have to be fearless, but you have to be willing to be afraid.

Suggested Next Steps

As you work towards happiness using the map of Self Discovery, consider taking some of these steps in your daily life:

- Take an online personality test.
- Pay attention to your body's natural rhythms and notice when you're most alert and most tired.
- Do the things you like more often.
- Do the things you don't like less often.
- Listen to your favorite music.
- Read a new book from your favorite author.
- Write a journal entry about your earliest fear.

Looking for more action steps? Every week I share a new happiness challenge online. These tiny assignments are based on science, research, and experience. Check out the latest challenge at http://inpursuitofhappiness.net/weekly-challenge/.

Map Notes

THE FIFTH MAP: ACCEPTANCE

"For after all, the best thing one can do when it is raining is let it rain."

— Henry Wadsworth Longfellow

"My happiness grows in direct proportion to my acceptance, and in inverse proportion to my expectations."

— Michael J. Fox

16

Acknowledgement Without Judgment

There are many ways to discuss acceptance. We can talk about accepting ourselves and accepting the people with whom we have relationships. So, too, can we talk about mindfulness and the acceptance of the present moment, of letting go of the past as well as the future. But first, we must take the time to define what, exactly, *acceptance* is.

Acceptance is acknowledgment without judgment.

It sounds like an easy thing, but we are not well trained in the art of observation. We observe-and-comment, all in one breath. Our language is filled with words heavy with judgment. A thing is fat or thin, better or worse, delicious or bitter. Attempt to describe an object near you and you'll probably find yourself habitually using adjectives that denote worth, beauty or usefulness. And it's damn near impossible to describe a person without revealing your own value prejudices.

One of the first things you can work to accept is the human

tendency to assign judgment.

It's just what we do. And we don't do it because we're bad people, or an evil species, but because judgment in many ways keeps us alive and efficient. Judgment tells us which berries will kill us (bad) and which will provide us with life-giving nutrients (good). Judgment helps us to avoid criminals and crimes. It lets us recommend and warn, encourage and protect.

But the usefulness of judgment, perhaps, has made us overly eager. We attach it where it's not necessary, and then we have to deal with all the feelings that are inherently attached to judgment. Those feelings spur reactions, and all too often we lose sight of reality or facts. We spend our lives sparring with smoke monsters.

Letting Go Of Normal

Depression is one of the smoke monsters that I flail at. One of the worst things about depression, for me, is the feeling that I'm not normal. Although my medication usually lets me live a totally normal life, there are still times when I'll struggle. When my depression flares up, I get tired easily, I can't focus, and I'm hyperaware of the fact that I can't do as much as *regular* people.

Because of the judgment I attach to depression and how much I am "supposed" to get done in a day, I get angry when the anti-depressants don't work "like they should." I worry that I suffer from laziness and personality flaws, not chemical imbalances. I question if it's my *fault*, then, and not something to be accepted and dealt with.

But depression cannot be managed with judgment. It has to be acknowledged so that steps can be taken to treat it. When I find myself no longer feeling healthy, self-loathing does absolutely nothing to make me better. I need to call my doctor, clean up my diet, make sure I'm getting plenty of exercise, and take time to rest.

I know that there are people, lots of people, who don't need to do a perfect dance with medication, food, exercise and rest. They don't have to think about how they're treating their bodies or their minds, and both just *do* what they are supposed to do. I am in awe of these people and their low maintenance bodies and I will probably always be jealous of the freedom they have, much like my envy of people who can smoke when they drink without becoming slaves to an addiction.

But I have to accept that I can't function that way. My body and brain are not, for whatever reason, that kind of normal. *This is my normal.* And every time I try to pretend that isn't the case, I will slip down the rabbit hole.

Courtney Carver of Salt Lake City offers another example of the importance of acceptance when it comes to taking care of ourselves. In 2006, a year after marrying the man she calls the love of her life, she was diagnosed with Multiple Sclerosis, a debilitating disease for which there is no cure. Naturally, her diagnosis caused her a lot of fear and anxiety. Her courtship with her new husband had revolved a lot around their mutual love of the outdoors and physical activity; she worried MS could threaten the very core of her relationship. But Courtney did not give in to fear or insecurity.

"I went into research mode," she told me. "I wanted to talk to athletes and people who were living well with MS." She combed the web and other resources for information about the realities of life with MS. In doing so, she discovered that stress played a big role in the progression of the disease. "I wanted to examine that and figure out how I was stressing my body."

Courtney worked hard to address her stressors. She

changed her diet, adopted a yoga practice, and embraced a minimalist philosophy. She adapted her spending habits so that she could quit her job, and now works from home as an author and consultant. "I don't think [stress] caused my MS – there is no known cause or cure – but it exacerbated my condition."

Amazingly, Carver says she is more physically active today than she was when she was diagnosed seven years ago. Her lifestyle changes are no doubt a significant factor in her ability to live well with MS, but it's important to recognize that those changes were possible because of her decision to accept her diagnosis. She didn't lose herself in a spiral of fear, but instead chose to educate herself on the realities of her disease. This acknowledgment of her normal let her respond rather than react, a difference that has allowed her to thrive.

Without Judgment, There Are No Flaws

In the book *The Beauty of Different*, Karen Walrond asserts that it is our differences that make us beautiful. She uses photographs to prove her theory that it is variety that makes the world a beautiful place, and we each contribute to that variety - and therefore beauty - with our uniqueness.

I'm fortunate to count Karen as a friend and mentor. Once when I was dealing with a bout of self pity about my lazy eye (oh, yeah, I have a lazy eye), she shared with me an epiphany she'd had while writing her book: There are no such thing as flaws.

As Karen reminded me, our perception of beauty is a social construct. What we perceive as "sexy" or "pretty" or "good" in terms of physical appearance is largely influenced by the society we live in. If you lived in the United States in the 1920s, you might have wrapped your chest in restrictive garments to give the illusion of being flat chested, because that was sexy. In the 1950s, you'd have aimed for an hourglass figure and spent your mornings using hot rollers to avoid the dreaded straight hair. While American woman today aspire to be thin, people in Fiji equate a larger body with wealth and power.

The rules of beauty are, in other words, completely made up. They are constantly shifting and changing, influenced by everything from capitalism to politics. It stands to reason, then, that the rules of what is ugly or unattractive are just as transient. What is considered a flaw today could be the height of beauty and fashion in the next decade. Karen asserts, then, that "there are no flaws, only differences."

Karen is right. The concept of flaws only comes about when we apply judgment; it's not an infallible declaration of the way a thing (or person) is. My lazy eye isn't inherently a good or a bad thing, it is simply something that may make my appearance different from yours, much like my blond hair or my five-foot stature.

Acceptance Is Not Perfection

A fear of arrogance used to keep me from acceptance. I thought that if I accepted myself for who I was right this moment, I would stop trying to improve. I worried that I would become a prideful person who clung to her bad habits and rolled around in self righteousness. "I accept myself!" I would declare, while completely ignoring anyone I hurt or offended.

I have learned, however, that acceptance has nothing to do with pride. I'm not suggesting that there is anything wrong with being proud of your accomplishments, but pride itself is a product of judgment. Because pride says that this thing you did was good (and maybe it was!), it's not quite the same as acceptance.

Acceptance is looking at yourself and being able to identify what you do easily and what you struggle with. Acceptance lets you admit that you can be impatient with the people you love, and that you lose your temper quickly when you're tired or stressed. It says that you easily make people laugh, and that you enjoy spending time by the water.

Acceptance says you quit your job without having another one, you flunked out of school, or you've been divorced three times. It doesn't deny your decisions or the consequences, but it also doesn't say that you're irresponsible, or a failure, or a screw up. It's your inner Joe Friday asking for "just the facts, ma'am." Acceptance is the moment of peace you grant yourself before deciding what you'll do next.

17

Accept Your Feelings

Of all my attempts at controlling the uncontrollable, perhaps the most futile and painful have been my efforts to control how I feel.

I don't want to have bad feelings. Anger, jealousy, resentment - I'm not so much afraid of experiencing these emotions as I am afraid of what allowing them in would say about me as a person. I worry that letting myself feel bad feelings would make me a bad person. Furthermore, the self-help books I've read have taught me that negative feelings are completely unproductive. I frequently find myself trying to *do* something about them.

My favorite tactic is to apply logic to my feelings. I tell myself things like "you shouldn't even care," and "it's none of your business!" For the record, this never produces the desired results. The harder I fight against my feelings, the more they end up controlling me. I get stuck in a spiral - I'm angry, and then I'm angry for being angry, and then I'm angry that I'm still angry even though I've acknowledged that I don't want to be angry. It's exhausting and becomes all-consuming. I have trouble concentrating on anything but what I'm not supposed to be feeling.

It's only when I finally give in that I have a chance of moving on. When I let down my defenses, the feelings I've been holding off often come flooding in. At first, it can be overwhelming. Pain, sadness, resentment - anything that triggers my defenses in the first place is almost guaranteed to be unpleasant once I allow myself to feel it. But then it begins to fade.

For me, it's like standing in the ocean and letting the waves wash over you. You know that there is no sense in fighting a wave; you can't hold back the ocean. But if you stand there and just let the water come, it will eventually recede all on its own.

Permission To Examine Old Wounds

I did not have a great childhood. My parents divorced when I was a baby, and my dad lived several hours away until I was in high school. My mother remarried a man who turned out to be very abusive, both verbally and physically. Although my mom and I were (and are) very close, I spent much of my early years desperately wishing my dad would show up and rescue me - and feeling horrible for wanting to abandon my mom.

Eventually, my mom divorced her abusive husband, my dad moved closer and made an effort to be involved in my life, and I grew up. I told myself that we all survived just fine, and so there was no need to rehash the past. After all, lots of people had way worse childhoods than mine.

And then I went to therapy.

I didn't go into therapy because I was mad at my parents. I went to therapy to try to find out if I wanted to get a divorce, and then to try and save my marriage. I stayed in therapy because I fell in love with all of the awesome changes I was seeing in my life because of it. But then, things started to get really uncomfortable.

It seemed I had some insecurities that were affecting how I made decisions. In fact, I seemed to have a pulsing river of evil slime flowing underneath the very foundation of who I was. That invisible ooze influenced my thoughts, my perceptions, my relationships, my reactions - nothing was immune to its powers. If I was going to really change what was happening up top, I was going to have to get into the slime and find the source.

As I dug - or rather as my therapist, Jen, pushed - I kept coming back to stories from my childhood. "This stuff is irrelevant," I insisted.

"Tell me about it anyway," Jen would say.

Still I resisted. "Dwelling in the past never changed anything. Yes, my father was mostly absent and yes, my mother stayed married to an abusive man for far too long when I was a kid. But we are good now. They've both worked really hard to make up for any mistakes. Plus, I'm an adult. I'm responsible for how I feel now."

I refused to betray my parents or present myself as a victim.

"I'm not saying anything bad about your mom," Jen assured me one day, "but she shouldn't have allowed you to live with someone who hurt you."

"She did the best she could," I said, a line I'd used to reassure my mother over the years when she'd tried to apologize.

"I'm sure she did, but it was her job to protect you and she didn't."

I left that session feeling extremely uncomfortable, a feeling that intensified when I saw my mom's number show up on my cell phone's caller ID. I considered ignoring it, but figured that would just validate my therapist's nonsense.

"How was therapy?" my mom asked. I usually loved sharing my insights with my mom after a session, and so it made sense that she'd be asking about my latest one. I tried to dodge the question as much as possible, but my mom has a knack for knowing what I'm trying not to say.

After a few minutes of me hemming, hawing and trying to "blah blah blah" my way out of an awkward conversation, my mom put an end to years of tiptoeing.

"It's OK if you're mad at me," she said.

"No, Mom, I'm not. You know I'm not, we've talked about this, and I know you did the best you could."

"I did," she agreed, "but I didn't do my job. And it's OK for you to be mad at me about that. I can handle it."

Saying that was one of the most generous things anyone has ever done for me. In giving me permission to be mad at her, my mom made it easier for me to let down the last of my defenses. Years of denial crumbled in the face of her humility, and I began to see what I'd been trying not to feel for so long.

Over the next several weeks, in the safety of my therapist's office (and sometimes in my bed at night), I let years of anger and sadness wash over me. I sat with the full weight of abandonment and came face to face with the belief that I wasn't loved enough to be saved. I cried a lot, but mostly I just breathed while the ache moved in and out of my chest. It was horribly sad and uncomfortable, but it was also extremely healing. It's a strange thing to heal wounds you didn't know you had.

What I realized through this process was that denying my feelings hadn't gotten rid of them. They'd been pushed to the side, but they still found ways to affect me through my insecurities and fears.

Feelings demand to be felt, and they will poke at all of your tender parts until you let them fulfill their purpose. The beauty of feelings, however, is that all they really want is that attention. Once they've been acknowledged, they tend to move along with very little extra prodding from you.

18

Accepting Now

My quest for happiness has led me to a deeper appreciation for the present moment, for what is right now. That acceptance has helped me to cope with pain, find beauty in the valleys of life, and ultimately be happier no matter what the day brings.

One of my favorite books is Eckhart Tolle's *The Power of Now*. It is not an easy read and more verbose and esoteric than I prefer, but he makes many points that are both profound and obvious. One of the themes of all of Tolle's writings is the concept of being aware of now. He writes:

> "Time isn't precious at all, because it is an illusion. What you perceive as precious is not time but the one point that is out of time: the Now. That is precious indeed. The more you are focused on time--past and future--the more you miss the Now, the most precious thing there is."

When I push past the flowery language, I see that what Tolle is talking about is my tendency to get caught up thinking a lot about the past or the future, especially when I'm upset. When life shifts, I remember fondly how things used to be and preemptively agonize over how horrible things will be from now on. Even when life is good, my obsession with time intrudes. I hold my children and find myself grieving because someday they will not be this little, and in doing so I squander the moment I'm preparing to miss.

We hear a lot about enjoying the present moment, and we're warned of all the happiness we will miss if we linger too long in the past or future. However, I actually learned the most about accepting now when "the now" was pretty damn awful.

On January 8, 2010, my younger brother Jay was arrested and charged with robbing banks. I know, right? Who gets charged with bank robbery in real life? When my mother called to tell me the next morning, she was laughing at how ridiculous the accusations were. "Can you imagine?" she said over the phone. "Jay cares less about money than anyone I've ever known. And apparently they think he's done it more than once, like he and his girlfriend are some kind of modern-day Bonnie and Clyde."

I laughed and told her to let me know when they got everything sorted out.

A few minutes later she called me back, and I could hear the death in her voice. I was turning left off Exit 92 onto Highway 436 in Altamonte Springs, Florida when she said, "He did it, Britt."

"What? What are you talking about?" She might as well have been telling me that her house had been invaded by extra terrestrials.

"They have pictures, from the banks. I saw the pictures. It's him."

"What?" I said again.

"He's wearing a wig and glasses but..." and she didn't have to say *I know my son*, because I heard it in her grief. "It was him," she said again.

I pulled into work, shut off the car, and hung up the phone. I looked out my window and tried to find a sign that the world had just shifted. I knew that it was turning, suddenly and violently in a new direction, because the movement made me want to throw up.

My entire world changed that day, as did the worlds of my mother, my brother Jay, and our baby brother Creed. Everything we thought we knew about good and bad and right and wrong and who the hell the people we love were - it all crumbled into a heap of heartbreak. I still don't have the words to explain the confusion and anguish that comes with being so utterly disappointed in someone you adore. It's unnatural to be angry at and grieving for the same person. And, deserved or not, it's a nightmare sometimes to stand by and watch the ones you love suffer through the consequences of their actions.

As we didn't know exactly what kind of sentence to expect, we swung back and forth between grieving for Jay as if we'd never see him again and hoping maybe he'd be in a halfway facility by the next Christmas. Because there is nothing fast about the legal system, even if you confess and cooperate fully with law enforcement, we spent two years waiting to find out how the story would end. Finally, in June of 2012, a date was set for Jay's sentencing hearing. His fate - and along with it, ours - would be decided in 48 hours. I spent two days trying to prepare myself for how I would feel during the hearing, after the hearing, if the judge said this, or the judge said that. I visualized the best and worst case scenarios so that I could practice my coping skills. By the time I arrived at the courthouse, I could barely breathe or see straight.

The hearing was postponed.

After all of all my mental rehearsing, reality met exactly none of my expectations. I felt like I had a basket full of possible reactions and not a single one of them was appropriate for the moment. I was baffled, overwhelmed, and a tiny bit grateful for the temporary reprieve on Forever.

It took a couple of weeks for a new hearing date to be set. In that time, I thought over and over again about how futile my emotional preparations had been. I reread *The Power of Now*, and I resolved to try harder to stay in the moment.

While we waited for the next sentencing date, I attended my daughter's first softball game, and I made a point of remembering how bright the sun was and how huge the batting helmet looked on her tiny head. I visited my grandparents and focused intently on the stories they told me instead of the old hurts I often bring into their home with me. I went to a drive-in theater and let myself laugh out loud at cartoon animals dancing in circus wigs.

When the day of the hearing finally came (again), I sat in the back of the courtroom and tried really hard to soak up each moment for what it was. I focused on the love that was shared by the people on the courtroom benches. I let myself feel the sadness of Jay's father, a man I have always had a hard time feeling compassion for. I even let myself be soaked in fear before I took the stand to give a character statement for my brother.

Make no mistake, that day was still hard. My brother was sentenced to "no more than 30" and a "mandatory minimum of 21" years in prison. But I felt like I not only survived that day, I lived it. And having the courage to live that awful, sad day made it easier for me to live the beautiful, happy days that have come since.

I try not to dwell on the fact that my brother will be in prison for 21 years; I don't need to borrow grief from the next two decades. I miss him when he's not at our family holidays, and I'm sad when I see his son experiencing milestones without his father. But I also try to be happy when I visit him, and to enjoy the absolute wonder that is having a two-year-old nephew. The only way I've found to survive this pain that's ripped through our family is to live it one moment at a time, and to simply accept whatever each new moment brings.

Practicing Acceptance

Accepting, like letting go, is an act we're often told to engage in, but rarely told exactly how. How does one accept the moment? How do we let go of the past and the future? To accept now, we must learn to pay attention to it. Like any action, there are specific steps you can take, and it gets easier with practice.

Remembering that acceptance is acknowledgment without judgment, what we practice is acknowledging, or taking note of what is, without adding anything else to it. You might have heard this described as being mindful or practicing mindfulness.

The act of mindfulness can involve sitting on a mat for a few minutes, but it can also involve doing any activity and paying attention while you do it. You can eat mindfully - pay attention to the taste and the texture of your food, and don't check your email between bites. You can walk mindfully - make an effort to notice your surroundings and the feeling of moving your arms and legs. It's not what you do that's as important as how you do it.

It's helpful to remember that mindfulness, or acceptance, is not about becoming a better person or changing who you are. That implies judgment. Neither is it about being able to zone out and shut off your mind completely. As Maia Dauer explains on her blog, "You may find that some of the consequences are that you become more relaxed and better able to deal with stress, but the practice of meditation is *not* about tuning out. It's very much a tuning-in and waking up process."

You just want to practice noticing what's happening in you head and in your environment, and try to break the habit of immediately needing to say:

- That's good,
- That's bad,
- That should happen,
- That shouldn't happen, or
- What will probably happen next is...

That's it. Keep your expectations low. Notice. Try not to judge. Notice some more.

I do find the "sit on a mat and close your eyes" method works better for me than other types of mindfulness. I'm not a good multi-tasker, and even eating while also being mindful can be one too many things going on at once. What I do is find a comfortable place to sit, outside if possible, and I set a timer on my phone. I started with five minutes (and this is where I restart whenever I get out of the habit of meditating daily), and then I close my eyes and try to focus on my breathing. As thoughts come in and out of my head - and they do, often - I make a point of recognizing them without holding on to them. More of a "huh, so there's that" than a "why can't I just clear my mind already!?!" And then I go back to breathing. I've also found guided meditation podcasts from iTunes to be helpful, as well as yoga videos.

Consistency is more important than how long you can be mindful or what format you choose. The more you practice noticing without judging, the easier it will be for you to practice acceptance in your day to day life. The key is to keep practicing.

19

Accept The Temporary

A word of caution: *the way things are* is constantly changing. Life is inherently temporary, and true acceptance must include embracing that temporary nature.

In the movie *Les Miserables*, the saddest part, to me, was when Javert, the hard-nosed parole officer, commits suicide. He has always seen life through the law, a black and white lens that cast rule breakers as bad people. When Jean Valjean shows Javert mercy and kindness, his world view is completely shattered. Instead of adjusting his perception of what is, he kills himself, saying that he cannot live in this world he doesn't understand.

While our lives are not a Broadway musical or Hollywood movie, it is not uncommon for us to cling to our perceptions and to even be wounded by our stubbornness. We'd rather die - or be miserable - than change how we see the world. And who can blame us? We decide who we are, what we believe, and how the world is - often after much soul searching and struggle - and then we attempt to navigate that world within those parameters. *And then the damn world changes.*

Culture changes. Normal changes. People you love do bad things and people you dislike show signs of common humanity. Life events like aging, divorce, or illness force us to change the way we define even ourselves. And as reality changes, the only thing we can do if we wish to remain happy is to continually strive to accept the latest version of normal. But that's a lot easier to say than to do, and it makes sense that this constant shifting of acceptance would take some getting used to.

Acceptance In The Sand

I met sand sculptor Rusty Croft on Florida's Navarre Beach. The local tourism board had brought in a handful of professional sand sculptors for a three-day event. Rusty and his fellow artists spent two days creating elaborate scenes in the powdery white sand, and their work was to be judged on the third day. My job was to write about the event and the destination.

On the second night, a rainstorm pummeled the coast while we slept. The morning of judging day, I found Rusty happily recreating the two days of work that had been washed out by Mother Nature. I was stunned by his jovial attitude and the lack of panic as he moved at the same deliberate pace I'd witnessed for the two days prior.

"Isn't this frustrating?" I asked him.

Rusty looked around at the now faceless sculptures he'd created. He shrugged and grinned at me. "What can you do?"

"True... " It occurred to me that even if it hadn't rained, Rusty's sculpture had always been bound for destruction. "Is it hard to make these things that you know can't last?"

He shrugged again, grinned wider as if he was deciding whether or not to share a delicious secret. "It's *all* temporary."

I must have looked startled. I *was* a little, truth be told. He'd just uttered a simple truth that seems trite when you read it on a slip of paper from a stale cookie at a Chinese restaurant, but one that's harder to dismiss when you can feel the proof between your toes.

Rusty told me about a tradition among Tibetan Buddhists that involves making elaborate sand mandalas out of colored sand with the express purpose of destroying them as soon as they're done. "Some of them take years to make", Rusty said. "And when they're done," he made a wiping motion, "gone. It's supposed to remind them that everything is temporary."

It's all temporary.

That truth is scary as hell, and it's something I try to forget when life is good. But there is also joy and freedom to be found in it.

When you accept that everything is temporary, you don't have to figure out what you're meant to do or what you'll be when you grow up. You don't have to try to pretend to know how things will turn out or decide what will make you happy forever. You can, instead, focus on sucking all the marrow from *this* moment. You only have to accept what is right now.

Trust Yourself

The realization that everything is temporary - both the good and the bad - can be terrifying. In fact, I don't think there is anything scarier than the idea of a dark unknown waiting for me somewhere out in the future. If at all possible, I try not to think about it. One of the benefits of learning to focus on the now is being able to ignore that shapeless uncertainty.

But when mental avoidance is impossible, I practice trusting myself. I run through a few doomsday scenarios in my head, and I picture myself surviving. I imagine being dropped in a completely foreign situation, and I see myself gathering the information I'd need to survive. I remind myself that I'm resourceful. What I'm really doing is assuring myself that I can handle whatever life throws at me. That is the key to accepting the temporary. It's not trusting that no one will hurt you, or that you've planned for every possible scenario; it's trusting yourself to be OK no matter what.

I don't expect to sail through life with an ever-present smile on my face. Nor do I expect never to cry again, never to make a mistake, never to be seriously pissed off at myself for having to endure the consequences of a bad decision. But I trust that I can muddle through until the tears have dried up, the time for penance has passed, and good days come again.

I trust myself to survive because that's what we humans do. We adapt. We move on. We change our definition of normal. We constantly find new reasons to laugh even after we've felt certain we'd never feel joy again. That's not hopeless optimism speaking, but fact. As humans, we are amazingly equipped to survive our new normals. Our brains possess a feature known as neuroplasticity, which means it can physically, structurally change in order to adapt to a new life. We are made to heal and thrive. I've no doubt you'll find evidence of that in your own life if you take a moment to look for it.

For me, my nephew Jude is a reminder of our ability to survive the unknown. We heard that Jay's girlfriend was pregnant just one week after his arrest. I was furious. My mind went instantly to all the added pain that Jay, his girlfriend, and this innocent child would inevitably experience. I thought of how things were supposed to be, and how I assumed they would be in the future. But when my nephew was born, I was compelled to let go of those future fears so that I had room to focus on the joy of that beautiful little boy. Babies are magical, I think. No matter what grief you've experienced, it's virtually impossible not to smile again at the sight of a newborn.

There is no way that we can know what comes next. We cannot begin planning or training, we can only practice accepting and being present so that we'll be able to embrace whatever life is going to throw at us. Change is coming, and our best hope of enjoying it is to focus on the now, and to trust that we'll be OK when the new normal comes.

Suggested Next Steps

As you work towards happiness using the map of Acceptance, consider taking some of these steps in your daily life:

- Listen to a guided meditation podcast.
- Take time to sit quietly for a few minutes.
- Consider your worst case scenarios.
- Make a list of changes and rough patches you've already survived.
- Try out a yoga class.
- Go for a walk and leave your phone at home.

Looking for more action steps? Every week I share a new happiness challenge online. These tiny assignments are based on science, research, and experience. Check out the latest challenge at http://inpursuitofhappiness.net/weekly-challenge/.

Map Notes

"I tramp a perpetual journey."

— Walt Whitman

Final Thoughts

As much as I've written about research, science, and the opinions of experts, I'd be remiss if I didn't tell you that they all pretty much agree that the greatest indicator of happiness is the quantity and quality of our connections with other people. If you have deep, meaningful relationships, you're likely to be happy. If you feel connected to your community and numerous people within it, you're likely to be happy. So why, then, isn't this a book about the five ways to approach connecting?

To be honest, I've always hated that part of the happiness equation. I remember reading once that the number of friends you had in high school was a reliable predictor of the amount of money you would make as an adult. It bugged me to think that my fate as an adult was set because I wasn't extremely popular among a group of 69 teenagers in the 90s. Similarly, I don't like to think that I don't have any say in how happy I am now.

It scares me to think that whether or not I am liked - and therefore connected with someone - is mostly dependent on whether or not someone else finds me acceptable. With all that going on in my head, it's no wonder I was so unwilling to admit the power of connections.

But it can't be denied. During the year or so that I spent recording my weekly happiness highlights, it became obvious that my connections to other people were most likely to inspire my gratitude. I was happiest when I was spending time with my family and friends, and also when I was forging new relationships. Similarly, I'm most likely to feel unhappy when I've spent too much time alone or I am feeling disconnected from the people who matter most to me. It's this need for connecting that prompted Jared and I to move our kids back into a home with neighbors, because we all missed that sense of community that is difficult to come by when you're nomadic.

Yes, happiness is connecting. But connecting is not, as I had previously feared, based only on luck, chance meetings, or the judgment of other people.

It's true that we only contribute to one half of a human connection. We can't control whether we will be liked or accepted, or even whether another person has room for or interest in making new connections. But we can decide whether or not we will show up, and that's huge.

I believe that the reason these five maps take us closer to happiness is because they prepare us for connecting. Knowing the boundaries of responsibility is essential to a healthy relationship with other people. Trying new things gives us something about which to connect with others, and offers us new excuses to leave the house and meet new people. Gratitude gives us open hearts, which is crucial for connecting. Self discovery gives us the wisdom and courage to present our true selves to the world, and acceptance helps us appreciate that same authenticity in others. This is how we show up and form meaningful connections. This is how we deepen our existing relationships. This is how we find the courage to branch out and form new communities.

But this is just the beginning.

As you begin to practice gratitude and experiment with doing new things, you will inevitably feel a new rush of happiness. This euphoria is impossible to avoid when you're stimulating your brain with novelty and stopping to count your blessings consistently. You may feel like you're finally getting in touch with who you really are; hopefully you'll like the person you discover. At some point, you will start to think you have figured something out, something significant and life altering, something you want to share with the world, or at least everyone you know. And that, my friends, is where you run the risk of becoming a colossal pain in the butt.

It's understandable. The hemorrhoids of happiness are formed from a sense of euphoria at no longer being miserable and a sincere desire to help. The sad fact is that most people you know (or at least a whole lot of them) aren't aware of the power they have to make themselves happy. You may start to notice how often your friends complain about other people, and when they do, it is tempting to point out how their troubles are really all their fault.

That will not go over well.

And the problem will not, as you might suspect, be that your friends aren't as wise or evolved as you. The problem will be that you're offering help when it is listening that's wanted. It can be hard to tell the difference, especially when you feel like you're walking around with the secret in your pocket to every unspoken problem.

The truth, however, is that you do not have it all figured out. None of us do. Furthermore, you are not the keeper of a universal key to happiness. Hopefully you've begun to figure out what makes you happy, but you must never forget that happiness is personal. Also, it is the unlocking of that individual mystery that really creates long-lasting happiness. You wouldn't want to take away the triumph of self discovery from someone else, even if you could.

Because I am unusually obsessed with things like personal growth and self development, I tend to assume that anyone who doesn't have a collection of self-help books is simply uninterested in and therefore incapable of embarking on the inner journey to happiness. They need my help! I suspect this is how marathon runners feel when they see me using my perfectly good legs to walk into a Baskin Robbins.

But I have to remember that I willfully choose 31 flavors of gluttony over physical fitness, not because I'm lacking the intelligence or willpower, or even because I suffer from some delusion that ice cream is better for me than kale and exercise. I choose to walk past the gym and into the ice cream store because that's where my priorities are right now. Should I reach a point in my life when that is no longer the case (and I suspect that day is coming soon), then I will make the necessary changes. I may even seek out advice or encouragement from my fit friends – the ones who weren't giving me unrequested ab rollers for Christmas.

Similarly, there are people in your life who may not be prioritizing personal happiness right now. They might have other stuff going on, or their current level of happiness may be serving them just fine. They don't need you telling them they're doing it wrong. If something changes, however, they might start looking to people who live happily for advice. In the meantime, the best thing you can do is have the guts to be happy for yourself.

There's No End In Sight

My friends have been encouraging me to write a book for a while. I wanted to write *this* book for months before I finally started. I worried if I was good enough and I stressed about donating time to something I might not do well, but my biggest obstacle to writing this book was that I couldn't get comfortable with the idea of putting myself out there as a happiness expert.

I still fall on my face. I still whine about life not being fair. I still break up with friends, fight with my husband, and want someone else to tell me how to make everything better. I have yet to reach the summit of Mount Happily Ever After, mostly because there is no such thing.

Happiness is not a linear path, but rather a circular journey along which we are constantly learning. We don't learn it once, check it off the list and move onto the next chapter. We come back to the same lessons repeatedly, bringing with us a little bit more experience and wisdom than the last time we encountered them.

Remember that there is no straight line to happiness. Happiness is not a place you arrive at, even with the most accurate map. There will be times when it seems you are moving towards happiness, and others when you're drifting away from it. That's normal and healthy and not at all something you can prepare yourself for.

Pursuing happiness often means walking the same road over and over again, and feeling like you're making no progress towards or away from anything. This is an illusion. Erase from your mind the image of a country road across a great plain and think instead of a path that winds around a mountain. As you make your way towards the top, you might take a look out over the horizon from time to time and think that you've been in this spot before. But you are not in the same spot; you are on the same side of the mountain, a little higher up than you were the last time you came around. The view is a little different, the perspective changed slightly because of the experiences behind you.

Know that taking responsibility for your life and your happiness is not about mastering life. Nor is it about eliminating all of your bad habits or becoming a perfect person. The point of this book is not to help you arrive anywhere. The goal is simply to put you behind the wheel.

Be patient with yourself, and enjoy the ever-shifting scenery.

Acknowledgments

I feel like I have waited my entire life to write this section. Finishing this book isn't just the result of a long writing process, but of a living process that has required much more than editorial support.

Of course, this book wouldn't exist without editorial support, either, and for that I have to offer buckets of thanks to Megan Gordon, as well as Faiqa Khan, Samantha Bennett, and Jennifer Pattison. You have each given me so much more than grammar tips and copy notes. I'd also like to thank Meri, Loukia, Deanna, Heidi, and Judy for giving their time to the unpolished drafts. And to Lisa: I appreciate you trying, but even more appreciate the hair patting, hand holding, and world-class example of friendship.

Thank you to Nataly Kogan, Christine Carter, Bill Rosseau, Rachel Jonat, Elizabeth Liu, Courtney Carver, and Maia Duerr for sharing your stories with me when it still wasn't exactly clear what I might do with them. Thank you to Rachel and Roger Reynolds for opening your home, and to Barbara Weibel for opening your heart. And especially thank you to Karen Walrond, for insisting that I take myself seriously when I asked you to paint words on me at BlogHer Chicago.

Thank you to Becky for showing me what happiness looks like and helping me discover Pittsburgh.

Thank you to the women of Propelle, especially Emily, Kate, and Carrie, for helping me push through the tears and the being overwhelmed. This book would still be a file on my computer if it hadn't been for your coaching.

Sheila Sellers-Harvey, thank you for being the face I see almost every time I sit down at the keyboard. Your open heart, courage, and strength to become exactly who you want to be have inspired me over and over again to keep going. And thank you to everyone who has read and commented on my blog over the years; you gave me hope that all the words mattered and that someone out there was walking a similar path.

Jessica Uhlenhopp and Erin Good, I have loved you both since before those were your names, and your faith in me years ago when I took my first big, scary step away from our hometown made this latest scary step seem possible. Also, you make beautiful babies and I miss you all so, so much.

Speaking of babies, mine are the most beautiful ever born, even though they no longer look like babies. Devin, I am proud of your wisdom and grateful for the way being your mother has transformed me. Emma, I am forever in awe of your natural ability to find happiness. Both of you: thank you for getting off the computer or putting on headphones every time I asked so that I could write this book.

Someday someone will invent a phrase bigger than thank you, and until then I will lack the vocabulary worthy of my mom and my husband.

Mom, you have always been my biggest cheerleader, and

your relentless vision of me as capable has allowed me to do more than I ever could have on my own. I am so lucky to have you as my mother, and thrilled that you are finally as much my best friend as I have been yours.

And then there is Jared. Honey, I want to say exactly the right thing here so that you will finally get just how much I adore you and how extraordinarily grateful I am to you, but I know that if I spend hours trying to do that and you say, "Oh, that's nice," then I will be crushed because you didn't cry and we will have a ridiculous argument ending with me saying, "No, really, it's fine. Whatever." So instead, I'll just say thank you, and I love you, and you are everything. I want to grow old with you.

About The Author

Britt Reints has survived a near-divorce, countless hours of therapy, and 10 months spent driving around America in an RV with her husband and two kids. Her essays on life and happiness have appeared in multiple media outlets, including Babble, Redbook, and Yahoo!. She lives in Pittsburgh with her family.

Connect with Britt:

- On her blog http://inpursuitofhappiness.net
- On Twitter @missbritt
- On Facebook http://facebook.com/ inpursuitofhappinessblog

You can follow news about *An Amateur's Guide to the Pursuit of Happiness* using the hashtag #HappyGuide on your favorite social media networks. This is a great way to connect with other readers and share your own insights.

31406006R10111

Made in the USA
Lexington, KY
12 April 2014